Alexander Graham BELL FOR KIDS

HIS LIFE & INVENTIONS

WITH **21** ACTIVITIES

Mary Kay Carson

CHICAGO REVIEW PRESS

Published by Chicago Review Press Incorporated
814 North Franklin Street
Chicago, Illinois 60610

ISBN 978-0-912777-13-9

Library of Congress Cataloging-in-Publication Data
Names: Carson, Mary Kay, author.
Title: Alexander Graham Bell for kids : his life and inventions, with 21 activities / Mary
    Kay Carson.
Description: Chicago, Illinois : Chicago Review Press, [2018] | Audience: Ages 9+. |
    Includes bibliographical references and index.
Identifiers: LCCN 2017027641| ISBN 9780912777139 (pbk. : alk. paper) | ISBN
    9780912777153 (epub) | ISBN 9780912777160 (kindle)
Subjects: LCSH: Bell, Alexander Graham, 1847–1922—Juvenile literature. | Inventors—
    United States—Biography—Juvenile literature. | Telephone—United States—
    History—Juvenile literature. | Deaf—Means of communication—Juvenile literature.
Classification: LCC TK6143.B4 C3695 2018 | DDC 621.385092 [B]—dc23 LC record
    available at https://lccn.loc.gov/2017027641

Cover and interior design: Monica Baziuk
Cover images: FRONT: Alexander Graham Bell in 1876, Library of Congress,
LC-G9-Z1-14931-A; AEA's *Silver Dart* airplane, Library of Congress, LC-G9-Z1-130,728-A;
Bell and his assistants flying a giant ring kite, Library of Congress, LC-G9-Z1-116,451-A;
Helen Keller and Anne Sullivan, New England Historic Genealogical Society; Bell's HD-4
hydrofoil, Wikimedia Commons; model of the first telephone, Wikimedia Commons.
BACK: Bell's liquid transmitter telephone, Wikimedia Commons; sign language and
tetrahedral kite illustrations, Lindsey Cleworth Schauer.
Illustrations: Lindsey Cleworth Schauer

Parts of this work were originally published as *Alexander Graham Bell: Giving Voice
to the World* (New York: Sterling Publishing, 2007).

Printed in the United States of America

5 4 3 2 1

Alexander Graham BELL

FOR KIDS

Contents

Time Line

1847 — Alexander Bell is born on March 3

1858 — Alexander adopts the middle name Graham

1862 — Young Alexander arrives in London to spend a year with Grandfather Bell

1863 — Alexander starts his first teaching job

1864 — Alexander's father develops Visible Speech

Alexander studies at the University of Edinburgh

1865 — Grandfather Bell dies at the age of 75

1865–67 — Alexander teaches and experiments with sound

1867 — Younger brother Edward dies of tuberculosis at age 19

Alexander's father publishes *Visible Speech: The Science of Universal Alphabetics*

1868 — Alexander begins teaching deaf students in London and studies at University College

1870 — Older brother Melville dies of tuberculosis at age 25

Alexander emigrates with his parents to Ontario, Canada

1871 — Alexander moves to Boston

1872 — Bell opens his School of Vocal Physiology

1873 — Bell becomes a professor at Boston University

1873–74 — Bell works on the harmonic telegraph

1874 — Bell has the idea for a speaking telegraph

1875 — Bell works on the harmonic telegraph with Thomas Watson

Bell begins building and testing a speaking telegraph, the telephone

1876 — Bell files his telephone patent on February 14

Bell hears Watson's voice over the telephone on March 10

Bell demonstrates the telephone at the Centennial Exhibition in Philadelphia

1877 — Bell Telephone Company formed on July 9

Bell marries Mabel Hubbard on July 11

1878 — Bell and Mabel's first daughter, Elsie May, is born on May 8

1879 — The Bell family moves to Washington, DC

Alexander Graham Bell at age 18. Library of Congress, LC-USZ62-115826

Introduction

An Inventive Teacher

The tall, thin man stood at the front of the class near a blackboard. His hair and whiskers were black and his skin pale. The dark suit he wore seemed well made, and a short necktie wrapped around the collar of his stiff shirt. He was dressed like many other London professionals in 1868. But the formal clothing made the young Scotsman look very serious and older than he really was. Alexander Graham Bell was only 21.

The young teacher picked up a piece of dusty chalk and began sketching on the blackboard. He drew the outline of a face from the side, in profile. He sketched a nose that jutted out, as well as lips and a jaw. The students watched in silence. There were only four children in the classroom. All of them were girls, and none was older than eight. But Kate, Nelly, Lotty, and Minna didn't blurt out questions or whisper to each other. The **sound** of chalk clicking and scraping across the blackboard echoed throughout the room.

Once Mr. Bell finished drawing the face's outline, he drew the insides of the mouth—teeth, tongue, and gums—creating a cutaway diagram showing the mouth's inner parts. Then he walked over to the children. The girls immediately stretched out their hands toward him, palms up. They weren't begging for candy or attention. The silent students were asking for an explanation. The teacher grasped a small hand and began touching parts of the palm and fingers in different combinations. The hand positions represented letters of the alphabet. This method, called finger spelling, was how people talked to the girls, who couldn't hear voices or other sounds. All four were deaf.

Mr. Bell first pointed to his blackboard drawing. Then he patiently finger spelled "inside of mouth" into the hand of each student. The girls couldn't speak either. There wasn't anything wrong with their voices. They could cry, scream, and make noises. But babies learn to talk by listening and repeating the words they hear. If you can't hear, how can you learn the sounds of words? In 1868, many people believed it was impossible to teach a deaf person to speak. But Alexander Graham Bell thought differently.

Students who were deaf learned to read, he pointed out. They knew the letters of the alphabet, obviously. It's why they could finger spell their thoughts. If deaf children could be taught how to make the sounds of each of those letters, they could put those sounds together and speak words, just like putting letters together when reading. How do you teach the sounds of letters to someone who can't hear? You show her how to shape her mouth so it makes the right sound. This was why Bell drew the inside of a mouth on the blackboard: he was showing the girls how to create the sounds of letters in the alphabet.

SEEING SOUNDS AND SPEAKING SUCCESS

IN THE small classroom, the girls were learning fast. They each touched their tongue, lips, and throat as Bell pointed out the mouth parts on the blackboard diagram. Next he drew a mouth making a particular letter's sound, such as *K* (*kuh*). The girls learned to speak the *K* sound by shaping their mouths just like the picture. Bell helped them practice the sound until they could speak it correctly. Then they learned the sound of another letter.

By the end of their fifth lesson, the girls knew all the consonants and some vowels. But letters can sound different depending on what words they're in. Think of the *C* in *cat* and the *C* in *cent*, for example. That's why Bell also taught the girls a special set of symbols, in addition to the regular alphabet. Each of the 34 symbols represented a different speaking, or vocal, sound. The sound symbol for the *C* in *cent* is the same as the one for the *S* in *sad*. The set of symbols for vocal sounds was called the Visible Speech alphabet. Alexander Graham Bell had learned it from the man who invented it: his own father! With this special alphabet, students who were deaf could learn how to say any word without ever hearing it.

Kate, Nelly, Lotty, and Minna worked hard with their young, talented teacher. They desperately wanted to learn to speak. They'd never talked with friends, parents, brothers and sisters, or neighbors. Soon eight-year-old Kate was able to say, for the first time in her life, "I love you, Mama." Bell had taught her to speak by seeing sounds. As an old man, he would write about these early lessons, saying

he "was thus introduced to what proved to be my life-work—the teaching of speech to the deaf." Alexander Graham Bell would work for the education of the deaf his entire life.

It's not what he's known for, however. The young teacher became famous for a very different kind of communication. In his late 20s, he invented a device billions of people use every day that instantly sends voices across thousands of miles—the telephone. Telephones forever changed how people communicate, erasing distances between individuals and connecting nations.

How did Alexander Graham Bell go from teaching the deaf to inventing the telephone in a few short years? How did a Scottish speech teacher become one of the most famous American inventors of all time?

The Bell family relaxing at Milton Cottage in 1855. From left to right: Melville James, Alexander, Eliza Grace Symonds, Edward Charles, and Alexander Melville. Library of Congress, LC-G9-Z10-31

A Curious Kid

1

Warm, sunny days are not something to waste in rainy, chilly Scotland. One late-summer day in the early 1850s, a young family was enjoying the fine weather in the countryside. After they ate their picnic lunch, the boys ran off to play. The middle boy was named Alexander and called Aleck. He was very young, perhaps three or four years old. But Aleck was already a fearless explorer.

A nearby wheat field swayed and shimmered. It caught Aleck's attention, and he set off to investigate. Once inside the forest of wheat stalks taller than himself, Aleck began to wander and wonder. *Does growing wheat make a noise?* The boy sat and listened hard for sounds of growing wheat, without any luck. Then he realized he didn't know how to get back to his family. The wheat was too tall to see over. Feeling lost and alone, and likely tired, little Aleck cried himself to sleep. "I was awakened by my father's voice," he later recalled. He sprinted in joy toward the sound of his father calling his name.

This was Alexander Graham Bell's earliest memory. But back then, he was simply Alexander Bell. He was born on March 3, 1847, in Edinburgh, Scotland. He was given no middle name but was named Alexander for his father and grandfather (with whom he shared a birthday). And the older men had more in common than just their names—grandfather Alexander and father Alexander were both expert communicators.

FAMILY TRADITIONS

As a young man, Grandfather Alexander Bell had been an actor. His training included **elocution**, the study of how to speak correctly—an important skill for an actor. In Grandfather Bell's case, it became his passion. He used his voice training to teach students with speech problems such as **stuttering**.

In 1833, after Grandfather Bell and his wife divorced, he moved from Edinburgh, Scotland, to London with his 14-year-old son,

ABOVE LEFT: **This photograph of Eliza Grace Symonds Bell, mother of Alexander Graham Bell, was taken sometime between 1880 and 1897.** Library of Congress, LC-USZ62-122257

LEFT: **Alexander Melville Bell, father of Alexander Graham Bell.** *The Canadian Album: Men of Canada, vol. 4, 1891–1896* by William Cochrane, John Castell Hopkins, and W. J. Hunter

Alexander Melville Bell (called Melville). In England, Melville went from assisting his father in his speech-tutoring business to being a talented speech teacher himself. But on a trip back to Edinburgh, 24-four-year-old Melville met the love of his life. Her name was Eliza Symonds, an Englishwoman living in Scotland with her widowed mother. Eliza was 34 years old and nearly deaf. Melville found her enchanting. He later wrote of their first meeting that Eliza had "the sweetest expression I think I ever saw.... She was so cheerful under her affliction that sympathy soon turned to admiration."

Though nearly completely deaf since childhood, Eliza spoke and communicated well. She used a funnel-shaped device, called an **ear tube**, to help her hear. She could also read lips some, recognizing the words people spoke by watching the shape of their mouths. She poured her energy into exploring the world through books, art, and music. She was also a talented portrait painter and pianist.

Melville was in love, and he and Eliza soon married. They settled in Edinburgh and had three sons: first Melville James (called Melly), then Aleck, and lastly Edward Charles (called Ted). Melville taught at the University of Edinburgh, published books on speech, and began working on something he called Visible Speech. It would become a universal alphabet of all the sounds a human voice can make.

Sound Beginnings

ELIZA WAS a talented woman in many fields, from painting to music. And from the time her sons were old enough to read and write, she added another occupation to her list: teacher. Eliza homeschooled Aleck and her other boys. She also taught them to play the piano. Aleck took to the instrument with a passion and quickly learned to read music and also play by ear. Eliza saw a special talent in her middle son and hired a famous pianist to become his instructor. The pianist believed that Aleck was good enough to become a professional musician. Music filled the boy's head day and night. Melodies ringing in his ears kept him awake at night and left him with headaches in the morning. His mother called it "musical fever."

Aleck grew out of his interest in becoming a professional musician. But he enjoyed playing piano his whole life—often late into the night. He later wrote, "My early passion for music had a good deal to do in preparing me for the scientific study of sound." It made him an expert listener with an ear that was sensitive to small differences in the tones and

········ Stuttering in the 19th Century ········

Stuttering is a kind of speech problem, or speech disorder. It's also called stammering. A person who stutters can't speak smoothly, or fluently. He or she can't help repeating or stretching out sounds or syllables while speaking. The flow of words is broken, choppy, or even totally stopped for a while. For example, talking like your teeth are chattering is a kind of stuttering: "Wha- Wha- Wha- What time is it?" Saying sounds for too long is another: "SSSSSSend me a note." Sometimes the speaker's eyes blink or head jerks, too.

Scientists aren't sure what causes stuttering, but it seems to run in families. Stuttering usually shows up when a child first learns to speak, between the ages of two and five, and it's more common in boys than girls. Most kids who stutter grow out of it. If not, a speech therapist can help teach people ways to speak and breathe that lessen stuttering over time.

Grandfather Alexander Bell lived during a time of much research into the causes and treatment of stuttering. In 1817, the French physician Jean Itard wrongly claimed that a weakness of the tongue and larynx nerves caused stuttering and recommended exercises to cure it. Grandfather Bell himself weighed in with his book *Stammering and Other Impediments of Speech*, published in 1836. His treatment methods included training the stutterer in breath management and relaxation. He also taught students how the vocal organs produced sounds so they could pay attention while speaking and control the process.

loudness of sounds. Studying, playing, and enjoying music also added to the special bond between Aleck and his pianist mother.

Eliza listened to herself or others play the piano with her ear tube or ear trumpet. She'd set its wide mouthpiece on the piano's soundboard, where the strings were located. Then the narrow end of the ear tube went in her ear. This focused and carried the sound into her ear, like a funnel. When someone wanted to speak to Eliza, he or she would shout into the mouthpiece. But Aleck had his own, quieter way of communicating with his mother. He learned that if he spoke to her in a low voice very close to her forehead, she could "hear" what he said. He reasoned that she was actually feeling the vibrations of his speech, not hearing sounds. For Aleck, this was quite a breakthrough.

Eliza also taught all her sons a finger spelling alphabet that used a speaker's hand positions placed on a listener's open palm. When Aleck spelled out whole conversations to his mother, she didn't need to use her ear tube. She could understand the words by feeling them spelled into her hand while also watching him speak.

An Inventive Youth

EDINBURGH WAS a modern industrial city during Aleck's youth. Steamships and trains sped passengers from place to place. Telegraph wires carried important messages, and factories and mills churned out newfangled goods. A number of inventions came out of Edinburgh, including the iron steamship and the pedal bicycle. It was an exciting time of new inventions—from photography to indoor toilets—that changed people's everyday lives. Thinkers, writers, and scientists of all kinds lived in Edinburgh, and many were frequent visitors and welcome guests in the Bell home. The Bells were among those who believed that education and new technologies made life better for everyone.

········ Sound Science ········

Clang! Woof-woof! Click-click-click. A sound is a sensation that is heard. It's sensory information taken in by ears. Like all senses, our sense of hearing is centered in the brain, which processes the received information into what we hear.

Sounds are caused by vibrations. When an object vibrates, it moves back and forth a tiny amount, causing whatever is around the object (air, water, Jell-O, etc.) to also vibrate, creating sound. Sound travels outward from the vibrating object in waves. Think of the waves coming off a pebble dropped in water, but in three dimensions like an inflating round balloon. The vibrating object pushes on the air around it, compressing the air molecules, which bump up against the air molecules next to them, and so on. When the waves of vibrating air molecules reach the organs inside a person's ear, they are translated into nerve impulses and shuttled to the brain. That's when the sound is heard.

MAKE AN EAR TRUMPET

Alexander Graham Bell's mother was nearly deaf. Eliza Bell used a device called an ear tube, ear horn, or ear trumpet to improve her hearing. These devices were common hearing aids during her lifetime. A person held the narrow end of a kind of funnel to his or her ear while aiming the wide end toward the speaker or sound. Ear trumpets work by capturing additional **sound waves** and shuttling them directly into the ear. The device also blocks out background noise when a person speaks directly into the wide part of the funnel. Make an ear trumpet of your own and find out how much louder a voice can be made.

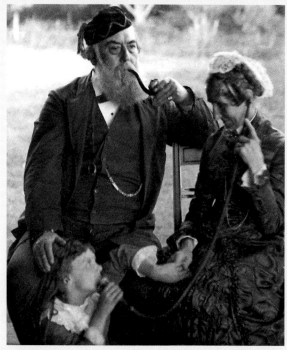

Eliza Grace Symonds using an ear trumpet to listen to her granddaughter.
Library of Congress, LC-G9-Z3-156,501-AB

You'll Need

- Paper
- Tape
- Radio, television, or a friend

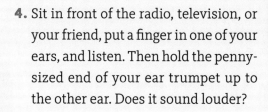

1. Roll the paper into a simple cone. The opening on one end should be about the size of penny, not a closed point. Make the other end as large as possible.

2. Tape it up so the cone keeps its shape. This is your ear trumpet!

3. Tune in to the radio, turn on the television, or ask a friend to help you. Your ear trumpet will work better with people speaking than with music.

4. Sit in front of the radio, television, or your friend, put a finger in one of your ears, and listen. Then hold the penny-sized end of your ear trumpet up to the other ear. Does it sound louder?

DO MORE: Have a kitchen funnel and some hose or tubing? Attach them to make an ear tube. Hold the free end of the hose to one ear while holding the paper cone to the other. Then repeat steps 3 and 4 above. How does the ear tube compare to the paper cone?

Life in the Bell household was fairly formal. The boys were expected to dress nicely and behave themselves indoors. But the Bells owned a country cottage in nearby Trinity, where the boys could hike the hills in old clothes and get as dirty as they liked. Aleck spent his free time at the country home collecting plants, studying animals, and riding an old-fashioned giant bicycle-like contraption called a velocipede. "Milton Cottage at Trinity was my real home in childhood," he wrote, looking back on those years.

Aleck liked his alone time. "In boyhood…I have spent many happy hours lying among the heather on the Scottish hills—breathing in the scenery around me with a quiet delight that is even now pleasant for me to remember," he later wrote. But Aleck spent time with friends, too. He'd met his friend Ben Herdman when Ben came to have his

FEEL THE SOUND VIBRATIONS

How could Aleck's mother Eliza "hear" her son's words when he spoke low and close to her forehead? Try this activity and see for yourself how sound is carried through bones and muscle to the ears.

You'll Need

- Earplugs
- Analog watch that ticks

1. Put the earplugs in your ears.

2. Hold the ticking watch by its band and place it against your forehead. Don't touch the watch face with your fingers. Can you hear the ticking?

3. Repeat step 2 on the top, back, and each side of your head. Is the ticking as loud on each part of the skull? Are some places louder?

4. Repeat step 2 with the watch on your chin. Is the ticking quieter? The sound has to move through the muscles that attach to your jaw to reach the skull and ears.

stutter corrected by Aleck's father, Melville. Ben's father owned an old mill, where the two friends spent hours exploring and playing among the stacked bags of flour and ancient grinding machinery.

One day, Aleck and Ben kept getting into mischief at the mill. Mr. Herdman got irritated with the troublemaking pair; he finally called them into his office and told them to find something useful to do. Aleck asked him what they might do that would be useful. After thinking a moment, the **miller** picked up a handful of harvested grain still covered in thick husks. "If only you could take the husks off this wheat, you would be doing something useful indeed," Mr. Herdman suggested.

The boys took up the challenge. First they tried scraping off the wheat husks with a stiff brush used to clean nails. It worked, but it took a long time by hand. They needed to make the work go faster. Aleck remembered seeing a big vat, or tub, in the mill that had rotating paddles in it. He figured that if they lined the wall of the vat with stiff brushes, the paddles would push the grain against them and clean off their husks. "It was a proud day for us when we boys marched into Mr. Herdman's office, presented him with our

An illustration from an 1875 guide to Edinburgh, Scotland. *Paterson's Guide to Edinburgh* by William Paterson/Wikimedia Commons

········ Finger Spelling ········

People who are deaf have been spelling out words with their fingers and hands for hundreds of years. Finger spelling uses hand positions to represent the letters of the alphabet. The speaker spells out words using the hand positions for a listener to see or feel.

There are many different finger spelling, or **manual**, alphabets. Some are as simple as tracing out the shape of the letter in the air or on the listener's palm. Most of the world's languages have their own distinct manual alphabets. In the American finger spelling system, letters of the English alphabet are formed by manipulating the fingers of one hand into specific positions and motions. The British finger spelling system forms letters using two hands. Eliza and Aleck Bell used a two-handed manual method similar to today's British finger spelling alphabet, except that letters were signed on the listener's palm. Not having to watch the speaker's hands meant they could look at each other's faces while communicating. People who are both deaf and blind finger spell into the listener's palm.

TALK TO THE HAND! LEARN A MANUAL ALPHABET

Manual alphabets use hand positions to represent each letter of a spelled-out message. It's just like texting! There are a number of manual alphabets in the world. Nearly every language has at least one. English has a British and an American version. Eliza Bell taught her son a two-handed version, similar to today's British one. Today's American version is single-handed.

Most people today use sign language to speak without sound. It's a system of gestures that represent whole words or concepts, so it is faster than spelling out each word. But manual alphabets are still needed to say names of people and places, and other words that aren't in sign language.

You'll Need

- Enlarged copy of page 8 or 9
- 26 index cards or 26 squares of card stock
- Scissors
- Glue or tape
- Pen or pencil
- Mirror (optional)

American Manual Alphabet

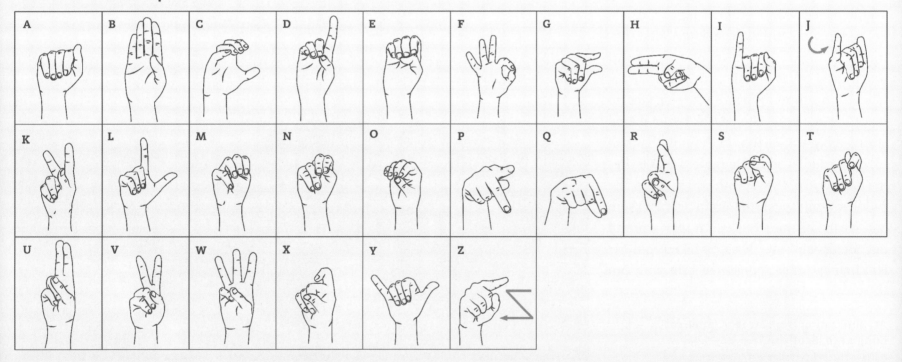

1. Choose a manual alphabet. The Bells used the British one below. The American one is used in the United States today.

2. Make an enlarged copy of your chosen alphabet. You can snap a picture of it and then print it out bigger, or enlarge it on a photocopier. The hands on the sketches should be big enough to see easily but small enough to fit on an index card or card stock square—about 1 to 2 inches (3 to 5 cm) tall.

3. Cut out the hand diagram for letter *A*, but don't include the *A* label. Glue or tape it onto an index card or paper square. Write the letter *A* on the back.

4. Repeat step 3 for the remaining letters. Now you have flashcards.

5. Use the flashcards to learn the manual alphabet you chose. Practicing in a mirror helps! Invite a friend to do the same. Then the two of you can spell out silent messages to each other.

DO MORE: Repeat steps 1 through 5 with the other manual alphabet. Not many people in the United States know British finger spelling. That makes it a great secret code between friends.

British Manual Alphabet

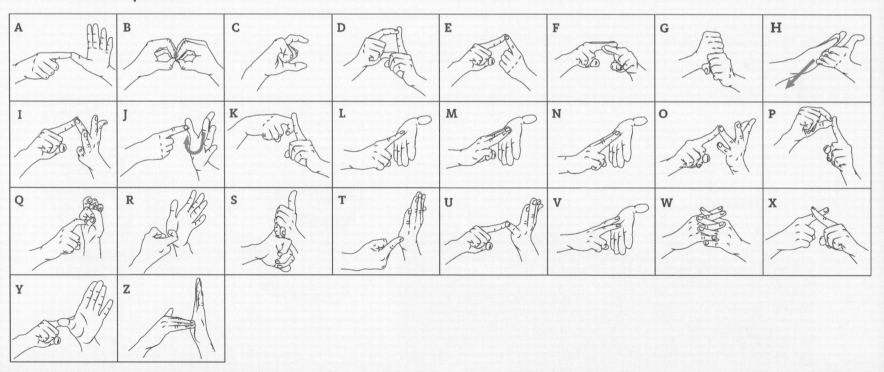

sample of cleaned wheat, and suggested paddling wheat" in an old vat, he later said.

The miller put the boys' idea into action—and it worked. Aleck's first invention was a success! Alexander Graham Bell wrote many years later, "Mr. Herdman's injunction to do something useful was my first incentive to invention, and the method of cleaning wheat the first fruit."

A Careless Student

ALECK FELT a bit invisible sandwiched between an older and a younger brother. He decided a middle name would make him more distinct and boost his individuality. There were a lot of Alexanders in his family, after all. Aleck took the middle name Graham, after Alexander Graham, a family friend. He later explained that "Alexander Bell was not nearly substantial enough to suit me. So I chose the **surname** of one of my father's former pupils, who had come to board at our house, Alexander Graham. It had a fine strong sound to it." The family embraced his new middle name, toasting him with it on his 11th birthday. But everyone continued to call him Aleck.

Aleck started Royal High School that year along with his younger brother, Ted. Their older brother, Melly, already went there. Melly was the best student of the brothers. Aleck was a smart kid, but he wasn't a great student. He was careless with math, hated learning Latin and Greek, and didn't even bother taking science classes. "I passed through... Royal High School... and graduated, but by no means

BELOW: **This 1844 picture of an early iron steamship is also believed to be the first photograph ever taken of a ship.** Wikimedia Commons

RIGHT: **A British advertisement for Victorian flush toilets.**
Wikimedia Commons

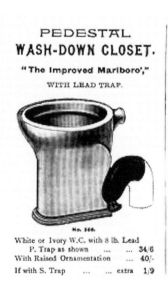

PEDESTAL
WASH-DOWN CLOSET.

"The Improved Marlboro',"

WITH LEAD TRAP.

No. 566.

White or Ivory W.C. with 8 lb. Lead
P. Trap as shown 34/6
With Raised Ornamentation ... 40/-

If with S. Trap ... ... extra 1/9

VALVE CLOSET.
With Basin and Slop Top in one piece, and Ventilating Union off Overflow Trap.

No. 568.

Valve Closet, with White Ware Flushing-rim Basin with fixed Slop Top, China Dish, 1-in. Supply Valve, Copper Air Regulator, Ventilating Union off Trap, complete as shown ... ... £4 7s. 6d.
If with 1½-in. Valve ... ... Extra 3/6
„ Box Enamelled inside .. ... „ 4/9
„ Box fitted with Brass Top ... „ 6/3

with honors, when I was about fourteen years of age," he later wrote of his less-than-spectacular school days.

Melville Bell was not impressed with his middle son's poor efforts and lack of focus. He thought Aleck needed to grow up and get serious about his future. And when a letter from Grandfather Bell suggested that Aleck come stay with him in London, Melville decided that this was the push his son needed. In the fall of 1862, 15-year-old Aleck left Edinburgh on a train bound for England.

BECOMING A YOUNG TEACHER

THE FIRST thing that Grandfather Bell did when his 15-year-old grandson arrived was call for a tailor. London in 1862 was the bustling, sophisticated capital of the British Empire, after all. Grandfather Bell took it upon himself to transform his grandson into an educated upper-class Londoner, starting with the boy's appearance. One of London's best tailors soon had the teenager outfitted like a proper young gentleman. Whenever Alexander left his grandfather's Harrington Square home, he was dressed in a dark, well-tailored suit, with a tie, a top hat, gloves, and a fashionable cane.

Perhaps it was just as well that Alexander didn't have any friends his age in London. He couldn't really hike and explore dressed

up in his fancy new clothes. And there were no country hills in London anyway. Grandfather Bell kept Alexander too busy to miss his brothers and friends back in Scotland much. Alexander was quickly put to work reading the plays of Shakespeare and other serious literature. He also studied speech with his grandfather, learning how to precisely pronounce each word he spoke. Alexander also sat in on many of his grandfather's sessions with his

Eliza riding a velocipede in the yard of Milton Cottage. Library of Congress, LC-USZ62-117719

students, learning how to help those with speech problems.

Grandfather Bell was himself the son of a poor shoemaker, but his education helped him become a well-respected speech teacher. He believed that schooling could help everyone live better lives—even the poor and criminals. Solving poverty and crime with education was a radical idea in those days. Back then, a person's social class was pretty much set at birth. A banker's daughter didn't become a maid. A street cleaner's son wouldn't go to medical school. These were facts of life in 19th-century England. Alexander soaked up more than books and lessons during his year in London; he absorbed his grandfather's ideas about the world, too.

Grandfather Bell's impressive knowledge of all sorts of subjects made Alexander realize how little he himself knew. Spending time with the elder Bell motivated the young man to become a better person, to educate himself. Grandfather Bell allowed Alexander free use of his library and its books. Among those the teenager read were science books about sound. The once lazy student even began thinking about college.

When a year was up and Melville came to take his son back to Edinburgh, he found that Alexander looked, spoke, and thought like an educated young gentleman. "This year with my grandfather converted me from an ignorant and careless boy into a rather studious youth," Alexander Graham Bell admitted. "From this time forth," he later wrote, "my [friends] were men rather than boys, and I came to be looked upon as older than I really was."

Three generations of Alexander Bells, with Aleck between his father and grandfather.
Library of Congress, LC-G9-Z10-47

Sir Charles Wheatstone

Charles Wheatstone was an English physicist and inventor. His most famous work was on electric devices like the telegraph and tools that measure electricity. Together with William Fothergill Cooke, Wheatstone invented an early telegraph in England. It was patented about the same time that Samuel Morse invented the telegraph in the United States.

Wheatstone invented the rheostat, a device that varies electric **resistance**. A rheostat controls how fast electricity flows through a **circuit**. It's what makes a dimmer light switch work. Another of Wheatstone's inventions was the stereoscope, a 3-D viewing device still used today. The knighted scientist also invented a musical instrument called the concertina, a kind of small accordion.

A SPEAKING MACHINE

BEFORE RETURNING to Scotland, Melville went to visit a famous London scientist and took Alexander with him. Charles Wheatstone was a **physicist** who had reconstructed and improved a speaking machine originally designed by Wolfgang von Kempelen. Melville

FOLLOW THE FAMILY NAMES

Alexander Graham Bell, his father, and his grandfather all shared the first name Alexander. To cut down on confusion, Father Bell went by his middle name, Melville. Young Alexander was called Aleck and added the middle name Graham. Look for all the names that are repeated in the Bell family tree. Are there repeated names in your family? Find out!

You'll Need
- Paper
- Pencil
- Highlighter pens or crayons

1. Draw your family tree similar to that of the Bell family. Add dates if you can, but it's not necessary.

2. Fill in the full names of each person—first, middle, and last names.

3. Like in the Bell family tree, circle the name the person was called if you know it. If she or he was called by a nickname, like Aleck, write it in and circle it.

4. Look for repeated names. When you find repeated names, mark them with a particular highlighter or crayon color. For example, all the Alexanders in the Bell family tree could be underlined in red crayon; the Melvilles could be blue; the Elizabeths green, etc.

5. Do you see any repeated names through the generations of your family?

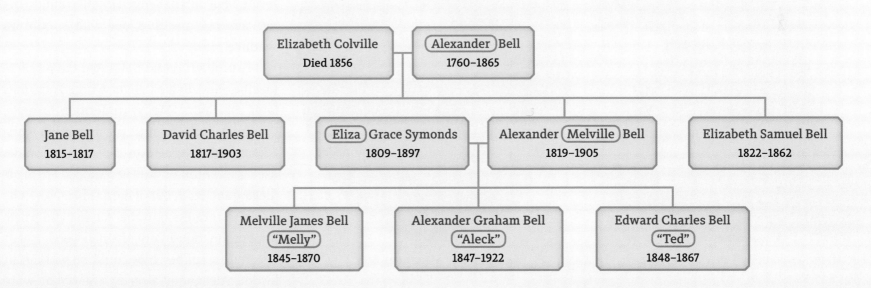

Elizabeth Colville
Died 1856

(Alexander) Bell
1760–1865

Jane Bell
1815–1817

David Charles Bell
1817–1903

(Eliza) Grace Symonds
1809–1897

Alexander (Melville) Bell
1819–1905

Elizabeth Samuel Bell
1822–1862

Melville James Bell
("Melly")
1845–1870

Alexander Graham Bell
("Aleck")
1847–1922

Edward Charles Bell
("Ted")
1848–1867

had heard about Wheatstone's speaking machine and wanted to see it for himself.

When the Bells arrived at the scientist's home, Wheatstone showed them a wooden box. On one side of the box was an accordion-like bag called a bellows, which acted like a pair of lungs. The other side of the box had levers and a leather tube that led to a vibrating reed. The reed made the box's voice, just like on saxophones and clarinets. When a stream of air hits a reed, it vibrates and creates sound.

Wheatstone pushed on the bellows, sending air though the vibrating reed while squeezing the leather tube and working the levers. Out came words! The speaking machine's words sounded mechanical and crude, but Melville was impressed by what he heard.

A year in London had made Alexander into a better student. It had also matured him into a young man. He had tasted independence living in his grandfather's home—and liked it. Melville had sent his son an allowance every month, and Grandfather Bell had let Alexander spend it however he wanted. But back at home in Edinburgh, the allowance ended. Alexander felt "treated as a boy again, after I considered myself a man." Older brother Melly, too, grumbled about living under their father's rule. Perhaps to distract his sons from revolt, Melville challenged them to build a better speaking machine, one with a more humanlike voice.

"My brother... and I attacked the problem together, and divided up the work," Alexander later recalled. "[Melly] undertook to make the lungs and throat of the **apparatus** while I made the tongue and mouth." Alexander used a real human skull as a model. He made the jaw and teeth out of hard rubber. Then he cleverly created a movable tongue and **palate** (roof of the mouth) out of small wooden slats covered in rubber that could be worked by levers. Alexander already knew that word

Alexander Graham Bell as a young teen.
Library of Congress, LOT 11533-3-50

Grandfather Alexander Bell.
Library of Congress, LC-USZ6-2009

pronunciation depended on how the tongue, lips, and mouth were shaped. Melly made the throat from a tin tube and the sound-producing voice box, or larynx, out of two sheets of rubber that met at an angle. After a lot of trial and error, Melly and Alexander put their halves together. Their speaking machine was ready to talk.

The boys took their contraption out to the common stairway in the house they shared with upstairs neighbors. Melly gave the machine lungs by blowing through the tin tube throat while Alexander maneuvered the lips, palate, and tongue. Out came a high, whiny voice! After a little practice, they got it to say "mamma" like a baby. "'Mamma, Mamma' came forth with heartrending effect," Alexander remembered. The upstairs neighbor came out to investigate, thinking she'd heard a crying baby. "This, of course, was just what we wanted. We quietly slipped into our house, and closed the door, leaving our neighbors to pursue their fruitless quest for the baby. Our triumph and happiness were complete."

Besides being fun, Alexander and Melly's speaking machine taught them a lot about how the human voice works. "The making of this talking-machine certainly marked an important point in my career," Alexander wrote in his 6os. "It made me familiar with the functions of the **vocal cords**, and started me along the path that led to the telephone."

SINGING STRAW

A vibrating reed was the source of sound for Wheatstone's speaking machine. The music of oboes, saxophones, clarinets, bassoons, and other woodwind instruments is also powered by reeds. You can make a simple version of a vibrating reed using a straw.

You'll Need

- Plastic drinking straws
- Ruler or pliers
- Scissors

1. Flatten about an inch (2½ cm) of one end of the straw. You can do this by scraping it with the edge of a ruler or crimping it with pliers.

2. Cut the sides of the flattened end like in the picture. The cutoff pieces need to be equal in size.

3. Does your straw look like this picture from the side? It should have two pointy lips. Messed it up? Repeat steps 1 and 2 with a new straw.

4. Make it sing! Put the pointy end into your mouth. Close your lips around it like you were using it as a drinking straw. Blow!

DO MORE: You can change up your straw instrument (or make others) easily. Cut out finger holes to make a recorder; make the straw longer or shorter to change pitch; add a funnel or cone of paper to its end and make it louder.

The majestic cathedral of Elgin was a must-see in Bell's time. Courtesy Bill Reid/Wikimedia Commons

Giving Voice to the Deaf

2

The speaking-machine challenge kept Melly and Alexander busy—for a while. But once the fun was over, the brothers went back to complaining about living at home. The teenagers wanted more freedom!

Edinburgh, Scotland, is on the coast of the North Sea. Alexander loved to visit the city's seaside docks and look out to the open water. A sailor's life seemed like a good idea to him; at least it was a way to escape the rules of his parents' house. He packed up his clothes and made a secret plan to stow away on a ship and work at sea. But he changed his mind at the last minute and decided to look for a job on land instead.

A job advertisement in the newspaper soon caught his attention. A boys' boarding school was hiring pupil-teachers. In the 1800s, a pupil-teacher was someone who taught younger students while also studying with the school's professors. Today it's often called a work-study program. Alexander applied for a job teaching music and Melly applied as a speech teacher at Weston House Academy in Elgin, on Scotland's north coast 175 miles (282 km) from the Bell home in Edinburgh.

Teenaged Alexander Graham Bell was a London-polished young gentleman.
Library of Congress, LC-G9-Z4-116,787-T

Eliza and Melville didn't know their sons were looking for jobs—not until the school's principal contacted Melville. The boys had listed their father as a reference, someone who could recommend their work. A family meeting was called to decide each boy's fate. The Bell parents declared that Melly would be sent to the University of Edinburgh for a year. Alexander would take a pupil-teacher job at Weston House Academy.

Alexander left home for Elgin and his first job. He was just 16. Weston House paid him only £10 (about $75) per year for teaching music and speech. But he also got a place to live, meals, and free Greek and Latin lessons. As it turned out, some of Alexander's students were older than he was. They probably had no clue he was so young though. Instructor Bell was a tall, serious, dark-haired young man who dressed in fine London suits and a top hat. No one confused him with the boarding school boys.

SEEING HOW TO SPEAK

ALEXANDER LIKED being a pupil-student at Weston House Academy. Elgin was much smaller than Edinburgh, and he enjoyed exploring the town, its nearby caves, and the rugged coastline. He turned out to be a terrific teacher, too. In June 1864, at the end of his first teaching year, the faculty at Weston was impressed. Alexander's students had aced their exams and earned high grades. The boy who had been a lousy student had grown into an excellent instructor.

With exams over, school was out until autumn, so Alexander headed back to Edinburgh for the summer break. When he arrived at the Bell home, he learned that he wasn't the only one having a successful year. His father had finally solved a professional puzzle he'd been working on for 15 years. Melville had finished the Visible Speech alphabet, a universal system of symbols that represented every sound of the human voice.

The first to learn the Visible Speech alphabet were Melville's three sons. Alexander mastered it in five weeks. He was a great help to his father when Melville set out on a lecture tour of Scotland with his boys. During lectures, Melville would give demonstrations of the Visible Speech alphabet in action. First he would have one of his sons leave the lecture hall. Then he invited a volunteer from the audience to say a phrase in a foreign language or an exotic name—something impossible to guess. As the audience member spoke, Melville translated the sounds into Visible Speech symbols on a blackboard. Next, the son returned and read the Visible Speech symbols aloud. Even though he couldn't understand what he was saying, it sounded exactly like what the audience volunteer had said. Audiences loved it!

Alexander Graham Bell later wrote, "I remember upon one occasion the attempt to follow directions resulted in a curious rasping noise that was utterly unintelligible to me." Alexander read the sounds on the blackboard

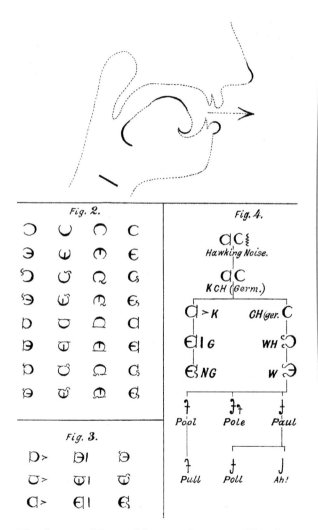

The face profile on this page from a Bell book on Visible Speech shows the vocal organs.
Wikimedia Commons

Visible Speech

Visible Speech is a way to "read" sounds. It is a system of symbols, called the Visible Speech alphabet. Each symbol represents a sound made by the human voice. It doesn't matter what language the sound comes from, or even if it's part of a word. Sighs, sneezes, grunts, and coughs can also be written in the Visible Speech alphabet. Each alphabet symbol represents a sound, not a letter.

Once people learned the sounds of each symbol, they could pronounce any word or sound written in the Visible Speech alphabet. The speaker didn't need to know what the word meant or what language it was. Only the sounds mattered.

The Visible Speech system became an important tool in teaching the deaf to speak. No one needs to hear the sound to be able to speak it. Today language experts use a system of simpler symbols called the International Phonetic Alphabet. But Melville Bell's Visible Speech was the first such system. His historic book *Visible Speech: The Science of Universal Alphabetics* was published in 1867.

This book illustration shows the names of simple objects written in Visible Speech.
Library of Congress, LC-USZ62-10442

aloud, but the result seemed more like a grating noise than words. "The audience, however, at once responded with loud applause," Alexander remembered. "They recognized it as an imitation of the noise of sawing wood, which had been given … as a test." The Bells put on quite a show. But the most inspiring use of Visible Speech was yet to come.

Sound Language

Sound science, or **acoustics**, has its own terms. Here are some of the basics:

● The number of sound waves that pass by a given point every second is a sound's **frequency**. (Think of it as how *frequently* the sound waves pass.) Sound frequency is measured in **hertz**; one hertz equals one vibration per second.

● **Pitch** is the highness or lowness of a sound. Pitch and frequency are related. Higher-pitched sounds have a greater frequency, so more frequent sound waves pass by per second. The lowest-pitched key on a piano has a frequency in the hundreds of hertz, while the highest key is in the thousands of hertz.

● When a particular object is struck, it tends to vibrate at its **natural frequency**. Metal, wood, glass, and other materials all have different natural frequencies.

● **Resonance** happens when a vibrating object causes another object with the same natural frequency to also vibrate. A singer can shatter a glass by singing the pitch with the same natural frequency as the glass. That's powerful resonance!

● **Wavelength** is the distance between one wave and another. Frequency and wavelength are related. A sound with a shorter wavelength is more compressed, so it takes less time for each wave to pass by, giving it a greater frequency—and a higher pitch.

● **Loudness** is a how powerful a sound is. **Sound power** is the amount of sound hitting an area—like an **eardrum**. The **amplitude**, or height of a sound wave, affects its loudness. Tall sound waves are the loudest.

Vowel Vibrations

"What are you doing, Aleck?" asked Alexander's irritated roommate. It was the middle of the night, but 18-year-old Alexander was across the room making faces in a mirror. He flicked a finger on his throat and cheek while seeming to frown and then smile. Alexander's late-night activities were keeping up his roommate at Weston House Academy.

While working on the Visible Speech system, Alexander and his father had debated why some vowel sounds were higher in pitch than others. A sound's pitch is its highness or lowness. A flute has a higher pitch than a tuba, for example. Alexander wondered if there was a connection between pitch and the vocal organs. Did different positions of the tongue, lips, and throat create a higher or lower sound? This was what Alexander told his roommate that night to explain his odd behavior. He was listening to the changes in pitch as he silently varied vocal positions and flicked a finger on his face. (Try it yourself. Silently shape your mouth as if you're saying *eee* and flick a finger against your cheek. Now try it with *ooh*. Which sounds higher?) He had discovered that the shape of the mouth and throat create the different pitches of vowel sounds.

His next scientific step was to determine the precise pitch of each vowel sound. He used tuning forks of different pitches to figure it out. Tuning forks are metal and shaped like a *U* with a handle on the bottom. They sing out particular pitches when struck, which is how they're used to tune instruments. Like anything that makes sound, a tuning fork sends sound waves into the air through vibrations. Alexander would strike a tuning fork, making it vibrate and sing out its particular pitch. While holding the singing tuning fork up to his mouth, he'd silently mouth the vowel sounds. If one of his mouth's vowel shapes made the tuning fork vibrate more—and therefore sound louder—Alexander knew that he'd found the vowel's pitch. This shared vibrating of sound is called resonance.

"Dear Papa," Alexander wrote his father from Elgin, "I have experimented again; and I find the general results of my former trial correct—and I now see the reason." Melville encouraged his son to write up his findings and send them to the scientist Alexander John Ellis. "At the age of 18 years I communicated to Mr. Ellis my discovery that in uttering the vowel elements of speech, faint musical tones could be heard accompanying the sound of the voice," Alexander Graham Bell later wrote. Ellis was impressed and persuaded

The Bells' United Kingdom

In the 1800s, the United Kingdoms of Britain included England, Wales, Scotland, and Ireland. (Only the northern part of Ireland remains in the United Kingdom today. The southern part, the Republic of Ireland, is its own separate nation.) Alexander Graham Bell was born in Edinburgh, Scotland, and spent his early childhood there. But he and his family lived in other parts of the United Kingdom. Young Alexander spent a year with his grandfather in London, England, as a teenager. The Melville Bell family moved to London in 1865. Alexander Graham Bell was an instructor in Elgin, Scotland, and in Bath, England.

Alexander to join the London Philological Society, a group dedicated to the study of language and linguistics, where he could pursue his love of language and speech. It was quite an honor for a teenager.

TRAGEDY AND CHANGE

AFTER GRANDFATHER Bell passed away in 1865, his son Melville wanted to continue his father's work in London. The Bell family moved to England, settling in its capital city. Alexander moved to England, too, taking on a new teaching job at Somersetshire College in the city of Bath, about 100 miles (160 km) from London.

Besides teaching students and taking classes himself, Alexander kept experimenting.

DECODING SOUNDS

Melville's Visible Speech alphabet is made of symbols, not letters. Each symbol represents a sound in language. The symbols themselves are instructions on how to shape and move the vocal organs—the tongue, lips, throat, and mouth—that create vocal sounds. A Visible Speech symbol is a kind of code that instructs the speaker how to make its sound. Different parts of each symbol tell how to shape the tongue, lips, throat, and mouth. Here are two examples:

- The horseshoe-shaped part of a symbol shows which part of the tongue to use. TRY IT: Say *tee* and *guh* and pay attention to where your tongue is. Standing in front of a mirror can help. Notice how differently your tongue is used?

- The up-and-down vertical line symbols describe how open the throat is. TRY IT: Say *eee* and *oh* and pay attention to your throat. Notice how different your throat feels?

Now take a look at the basic Visible Speech alphabet for English on page 23. It's separated into consonant sounds and vowel sounds. Notice the bold part of the sample word below each symbol. This is the part of the word whose sound is represented by the symbol.

For example: Ω
　　　　　ru**sh**

Ω represents the *shh* sound, as in the word *rush*.

Can you decode this phrase?

ᚠω ᙣᚦ⠙ᙣᙡ ᙃᚨᙖᙡ Ⴕᵥ ᚱᏳᵹᙓω

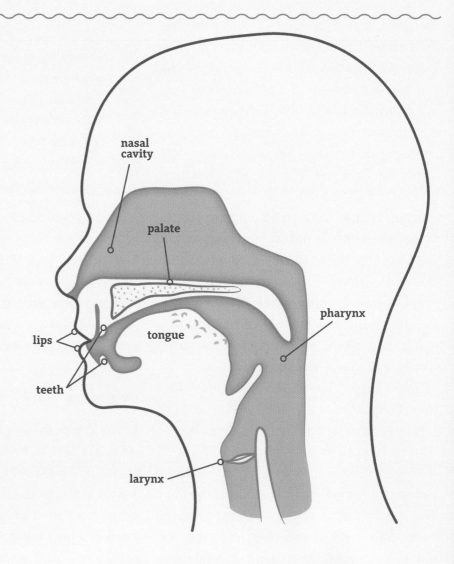

nasal cavity

palate

pharynx

lips

tongue

teeth

larynx

Write a message to a friend using the Visible Speech alphabet. Make it simple, such as: *See you at the game* or *Meet me at four*. Then ask your friend to write back in the code.

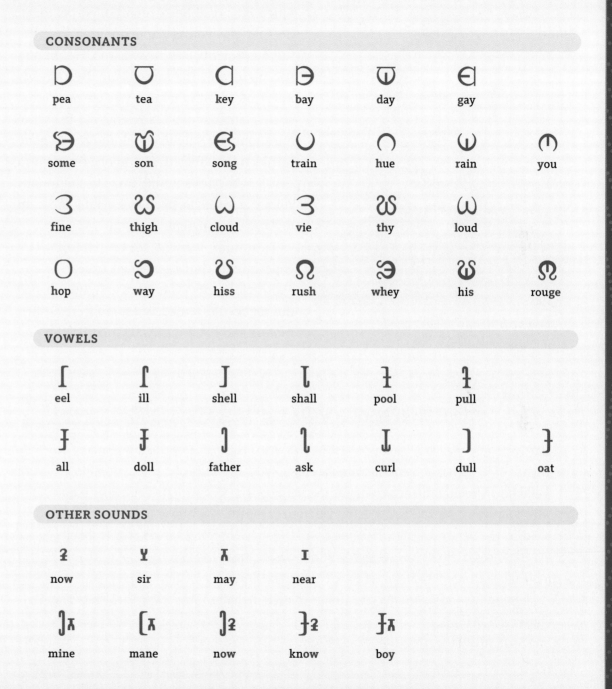

CONSONANTS

pea	tea	key	bay	day	gay
some	son	song	train	hue	rain	you
fine	thigh	cloud	vie	thy	loud
hop	way	hiss	rush	whey	his	rouge

VOWELS

eel	ill	shell	shall	pool	pull
all	doll	father	ask	curl	dull	oat

OTHER SOUNDS

now	sir	may	near
mine	mane	now	know	boy

All human beings are equal.

23

Alexander Graham Bell at age 18.
Library of Congress, LC-USZ62-115826

When Ellis read Bell's report on vowel tones, he told the young experimenter that the famous scientist Hermann von Helmholtz had discovered the same thing. Bell already knew of Helmholtz and was inspired that such a famous mind had pondered the same question. Ellis said that Helmholtz had gone further by building his Helmholtz resonator, a device that causes tuning forks to continually vibrate at a specific pitch by hooking them up to an electric **current**.

Alexander wanted to try Helmholtz's experiments, but he needed to learn more about electricity. The electric lightbulb had not yet been invented, but there were electric motors and batteries. And Great Britain and the United States had thousands of miles of telegraph wires shuttling electric messages by then.

Best to learn by doing, Alexander decided. He filled his room in Bath with battery-making supplies, including glass bottles, acid, zinc, and copper. He and a friend in a nearby boardinghouse strung wires between their windows, hooked up telegraphs to each end, and started sending messages back and forth.

But things were changing in the Bell family. Back in London, Alexander's younger brother, Ted, was very sick. His bad cough turned out to be a disease that infects the lungs called **tuberculosis**. Ted was bedridden all winter, only able to sit up for an hour or so at time. "So long as Edward keeps still, he is not much troubled with his cough," Eliza wrote hopefully to Alexander around her middle son's 20th birthday. But, as everyone feared, Ted was seriously ill. He died on May 17, 1867. "He was only eighteen years and eight months old," Alexander wrote in his diary that day.

Hermann von Helmholtz

Hermann Ludwig Ferdinand von Helmholtz was a German physicist. Like many scientists of his time, he experimented and studied more than one topic. Helmholtz's well-known book about acoustics, *On the Sensations of Tone*, included his experiments with sound that Alexander Graham Bell tried to repeat. Helmholtz also used physics to study the nervous system. He measured the speed of firing nerves, which are electric impulses. Helmholtz was an inventor, too. He made the first ophthalmoscope, a medical instrument that doctors use to examine eyes.

Helmholtz's most famous scientific work was helping to discover the law of the conservation of energy. The scientific principle says that energy can be changed from one form to another but that it can't be created or destroyed.

LIFE AND TEACHING IN LONDON

When the school year ended in 1867, Alexander moved home to London. He wouldn't be going back to Bath—even though he liked being independent. Ted was gone and brother Melly was now married and living back in

Scotland, so Aleck was the only son at home. How could he abandon his parents?

It wasn't a terrible change. Alexander had plenty to do in London. He went to college at the University of London and helped his father demonstrate his Visible Speech system. Audiences were amazed that Alexander could correctly pronounce a sound he'd never heard before by simply reading aloud the Visible Speech symbols. An old student of Melville's named Susanna Hull had a school for the deaf in London. When she learned about the Visible Speech system, she asked if it could be taught to her students. Melville sent 21-year-old Alexander to try.

Experts of the day claimed teaching the deaf to speak was impossible. But Alexander would prove them wrong. All his students needed to do was learn how to make the sounds of the Visible Speech alphabet. Then they could string the sounds together and speak words. The four young girls in Alexander's class were eager to learn to speak. They paid close attention to their serious instructor as he drew sketches of the vocal organs on the blackboard. He communicated with them by finger spelling into their palms, helping the girls learn to shape their mouths and lips.

After weeks of lessons with their dedicated teacher, the girls learned how to make the sounds in the Visible Speech alphabet. They learned to speak without ever hearing a spo-

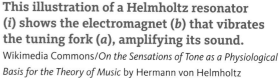

This illustration of a Helmholtz resonator (*i*) shows the electromagnet (*b*) that vibrates the tuning fork (*a*), amplifying its sound.
Wikimedia Commons/*On the Sensations of Tone as a Physiological Basis for the Theory of Music* by Hermann von Helmholtz

RIGHT: Batteries of the kind used in the 1860s were glass jars filled with lead and acid.
Wikimedia Commons

ken word. Teaching at the deaf school was the beginning of what Alexander Graham Bell would consider to be his lifework—teaching people who were deaf to speak. The young instructor quickly earned a reputation as a talented teacher of the deaf.

DEATH AND NEW BEGINNINGS

ALEXANDER'S YOUNG adult life was coming together nicely. Besides teaching and studying, he took care of his father's speech business in London when Melville was away. Melville had

SEEING SOUND

Sound is all about vibrations on the move. You hear a song once the waves of sound reach your ears. Shine some light on how sounds create vibrations in this activity.

You'll Need

- Round balloon
- Scissors
- Medium-sized (5–8 inches [13–20 cm] high) metal can, such as a coffee can or large soup can, with both ends removed
- Rubber bands
- Tape
- Glue
- Small piece of mirror (sold in craft stores)
- Old magazine or piece of cardboard
- Flashlight
- Friend

1. Cut off the neck of a round balloon.

2. Stretch the cut balloon tightly over one open end of the can. Wrap rubber bands around the can to secure the stretched balloon. Still slipping? Tape over the rubber bands to hold it tighter.

3. Glue the piece of mirror onto the balloon-covered top with the reflective side facing out. Set it aside to fully dry.

4. Choose a place that's dark enough to see the flashlight's beam. A windowless room or shadowed corner should work.

5. Turn the can onto its side. To keep the can from rolling around, tape it down onto the old magazine or cardboard piece.

6. Place the can setup about 2 feet (about ½ m) from the wall with the mirror side facing the wall.

7. Darken the room and stand between the wall and the can, but off to one side. Practice aiming the flashlight at the mirror so that it reflects a square of light onto the wall.

8. Ask the friend to speak into the can without touching it while you reflect light off the mirror using the flashlight. Does the light on the wall move?

9. Repeat step 8 asking the friend to yell or clap instead. Does the light move more or less?

traveled to North America to promote Visible Speech. While there, he visited old friends who'd moved to Canada from Scotland. Melville liked Canada and thought about moving there, too, but for now he felt he belonged in London.

Tuberculosis continued to plague Britain after the illness killed Ted in 1867. Now the sickness stalked Melly's family in Edinburgh. He and his wife, Carrie, sent a picture of their infant son, Edward, to London. It showed a "determined little fellow" with big eyes and clenched fists. But baby Edward wasn't well. And Melly was thin and pale, too. In early 1870, baby Edward died of tuberculosis at just over a year old. The loss caused Melly to take up spiritualism, the belief that the living could communicate with the dead through meetings called séances. Melly made Alexander promise that whichever brother died first would try to communicate with the other.

A few months after burying his tiny son, 25-year-old Melly died of tuberculosis on May 28, 1870. He was buried beside his brother Ted and Grandfather Bell in London. The death of his older brother devastated Alexander. "I well remember how often—in the stillness of the night—I've had little séances all by myself in the half-hope, half-fear of receiving some communication," he later wrote. He kept his promise of trying to communicate beyond the grave, though without success.

······ Consumed by Tuberculosis ······

Tuberculosis, or TB, is a lung disease caused by tubercle bacilli bacteria, which infect the lungs. Today, people with TB are usually cured with antibiotics and bacteria-fighting drugs. But there were no such medicines in the 1800s. It was nearly the end of the 19th century before microscopic germs like bacteria and viruses were even discovered.

This English school poster from the 19th century offers advice for recovering from tuberculosis, or consumption.
Wikimedia Commons

Tuberculosis was called consumption in Alexander Graham Bell's day. The name described how the disease slowly weakened the bodies of its victims, consuming their health over time. Someone with TB might spend months in bed wasting away before finally dying. The White Plague of consumption ravaged Europe during the 1800s, killing millions of people. It was the cause behind one in four deaths.

All sorts of treatments and cures for consumption were offered during the tuberculosis epidemic. This one claimed that electricity on the chest would cure the disease. Courtesy Wellcome Library, London, L0038314

Tuberculosis spreads easily when someone with the disease coughs or sneezes. People living close together are more likely to catch it and pass it on to others. Some patients did recover, though in the 1800s it took months or years for a person's body to fight off the infection and heal. Recovery homes for TB patients called sanitariums opened in the late 1800s to help cure patients with fresh air, rest, and good nutrition. Sanitariums also prevented the spread of the disease by isolating infected people.

FEELING SOUND

Sound is created by vibrations. Waves of vibrating air carry sounds to your ears. Sound traveling through air is invisible, but the vibrations of sound waves can be felt. Prove it to yourself in this activity.

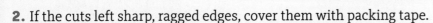

You'll Need

- Plastic soda bottle
- Scissors
- Packing tape (optional)
- Round balloon
- Rubber bands (optional)

1. Carefully cut off the bottom end of a plastic soda bottle.

2. If the cuts left sharp, ragged edges, cover them with packing tape.

3. Cut the neck off a round balloon.

4. Stretch the balloon tightly over the cut end of the plastic bottle. If the balloon slips, wrap rubber bands around the bottle to secure it.

5. Ready to feel sound? Hold the bottle with one hand while lightly placing the fingers of your other hand over the balloon-covered end. Bring the mouth end of the bottle near your mouth and say your name into it. Can you feel the balloon moving? Make sure you're speaking but not blowing into the mouth of the bottle.

6. Repeat step 5 with a loud yell or place the mouth end of the bottle near a radio or TV speaker. Does the loudness of the sound matter?

After burying two sons, Eliza and Melville worried about Alexander's health. He stayed up half the night and slept all morning. Was illness causing Alexander's fatigue? He often complained of bad headaches, too. Would the Bells' only remaining son die of tuberculosis, too? A trip to the doctor added to their fears. The doctor claimed that if Alexander didn't move someplace healthier to recuperate, he'd likely die in six months or so. Eliza and Melville felt that Canada was the cure Alexander needed. But could they convince him to go?

Alexander felt his dream of an independent life falling apart around him. If he moved to Canada, he'd never finish his college degree, and he'd have to leave his students at the deaf school. But how could he say no to his parents? They'd already lost two sons. Alexander was their only living child. He felt it was his duty to fulfill his parents' wishes. In a letter to them, he wrote that his dream of independence "has perished with poor Melly. It is gone and for ever … [and] I have now no other wish than to be near you, Mama … and I put myself unreservedly into your hands to do with me whatever you think for the best." It was signed, "Your affectionate and only son, Aleck."

A ship soon carried Alexander and his family away from Great Britain and across the Atlantic Ocean. It landed in Canada on August 1, 1870. Alexander Graham Bell had arrived in North America.

SOUND POWER

Sound travels in waves. Sound waves carry energy, which means they can exert force on objects. Just like ocean waves can move rocks, sound affects the air or other matter it passes through. See how concentrated sound pulses through water, making it move.

You'll Need

- Balloon
- Scissors
- Paper towel tube
- Rubber bands
- Tape
- Paper
- Pie tin or other shallow dish
- Water
- Food coloring

1. Cut the neck off the balloon and stretch it over one end of the cardboard paper towel tube.

2. Stretch the balloon tight and use rubber bands to hold it in place. Wrap tape over the rubber bands if the balloon is slipping.

3. Make a small cone out of the paper and then tape it onto the other end of the tube. Make sure there's a hole at the tip of the cone. You've made a sound cannon!

4. Set the pie tin or dish on a table and fill it about halfway with water.

5. Aim the cone-tipped end of your cannon toward the surface of the water. It needs to be close to the water but not touching it.

6. While holding the cannon steady with one hand, yell near the balloon end without touching it. Does the water move?

7. Quickly and carefully add a single drop of food coloring to the water. Then repeat steps 5 and 6. Is it easier to see the water moving now?

8. If you're still having trouble seeing the water move, try a louder sound like a radio or horn. You can prop up the cannon on some stacked books so you'll have free hands to knock pans together or blow into a trumpet.

The Bell family home in Brantford, Canada. Patent and Copyright Office, Library and Archives Canada Copyright, HS85/10/40416

The Bell Patent Association

3

Alexander Graham Bell and his parents arrived in Canada in the summer of 1870. The family moved into a home in Ontario. The city of Brantford sits between Lake Ontario and Lake Erie. The Bell family home overlooked the Grand River, and Alexander soon found a favorite spot to watch the water flow below. "It was my custom in the summer time to take a rug, a pillow, and an interesting book to this cozy little nook and dream away the afternoon," he later wrote. Alexander stayed nearly a year at his parents' home, resting and becoming healthy again. Moving to Canada seemed to be the cure Eliza and Melville had hoped for. Their only living child was no longer weak and sick.

A bustling Boston intersection in the late 1800s. City of Boston Archives, 14520231384

In 1871, a fully recovered Alexander moved to Boston, Massachusetts. He decided to once again become a teacher of speech to deaf students using Visible Speech. It was a good decision for the young, ambitious instructor. Within a few years, he advanced from being a teacher at a number of schools to a professor of vocal physiology at Boston University.

Alexander's methods of teaching deaf students to speak using Visible Speech received praise and attention in Boston. Newspapers reported on the amazing progress young Pro-

fessor Bell made with his students. Like the Alexander Bells before him, he also opened his own speech tutoring business. Bell called it his School of **Vocal Physiology**.

EARLY BOSTONIAN EXPERIMENTS

BESIDES TEACHING, Bell continued experimenting with sound as he had back in Scotland. He became fascinated by a recent invention called the **phonautograph**. The machine created the first-ever recording of sound. Unlike a tape recorder or MP3 player, the phonautograph couldn't play back sounds. It simply recorded a sound's pattern of sound waves. The recorded pattern, called a **phonautogram**, is a sort of "sound picture" that shows the pattern of sound waves. A phonautogram of someone shouting looks different than one of a bird singing. Today we'd call them **spectrograms**, those graphs of up and down lines on audio equipment that change as someone is speaking.

Bell thought a machine that mapped out sounds would be a great tool for students learning to speak. If students who were deaf could see the pattern of a word made by a phonautograph, they could use the pattern to check their own pronunciation of the word. Bell hoped that students could use a phonautograph to help them practice speaking a

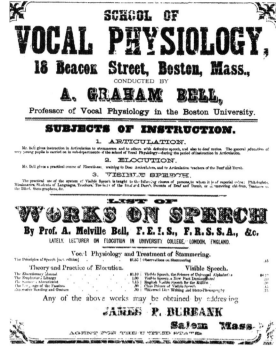

word correctly until the student's phonautogram matched the original.

Unfortunately, phonautographs weren't very sensitive back then. Small but important differences in pronunciation didn't really show up on the phonautograms. It was too crude of an instrument. Perhaps he could build a superior one, thought Bell, a phonautograph as sensitive as human hearing.

What better material to mimic human hearing than a real human ear? Bell obtained just that from a corpse for his attempt at an improved phonautograph. He attached a slender straw to one of the tiny bones inside the ear. Then he mounted the ear over a piece of glass covered in a thin layer of ink, like a muddy windshield. When someone spoke into the ear, the eardrum vibrated, set the ear bones in motion, and caused the straw to scratch lines on the inked glass. It worked!

Bell was never able to build a workable teaching tool for deaf students out of his human ear phonautograph. But it "paved the way for the

The Phonautograph

The phonautograph was the first machine to create a recording of sound. It was invented in 1857 by Édouard-Léon Scott de Martinville. The recording was called a phonautogram. It showed a pattern of lines scratched into soot-covered paper by a stylus, often made of a stiff pig bristle. The sooty paper was wound onto a cylinder so it could be turned as the stylus moved and create the phonautogram.

Someone would speak into the wide end of the megaphone-like tube, and his or her voice would create sound waves. These sound waves caused the thin **membrane** to vibrate. A stylus attached to the stretched membrane moved with the vibrations, scratching the vibrations' patterns—sounds—on coated glass plates. A visual picture or graphic of the sound was left behind.

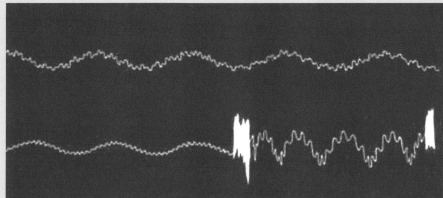

ABOVE: A phonautogram. Wikimedia Commons

LEFT: A phonautograph. *The Entire Natural Sciences* by Hermann Masius/ Wikimedia Commons

appearance of the first membrane telephone," the inventor later wrote. How so? It showed that spoken sound waves caused vibrations strong enough to move a thin membrane, like the tiny vibrating drumlike membrane of a phonautograph. What else might the human voice be strong enough to power? The answer was the other subject of Bell's early Boston experiments—electric current.

BUILDING A BETTER TELEGRAPH

BOSTON WAS a busy place in the late 19th century. The Massachusetts city was full of university students, scientists, and inventors. It was also home to rich businessmen in search of opportunities to make money. One such man was Gardiner Greene Hubbard. The successful lawyer was looking for new technologies to invest in.

Hubbard's daughter Mabel was a student of Bell's. Bell was helping the deaf teenager speak more clearly. Mr. Hubbard liked the young professor, and Bell was a frequent guest of the family. In the fall of 1874, Bell was entertaining his hosts with his piano skills at the Hubbard home. Suddenly he lifted his hands from the keyboard, stopped playing, and spun around on the stool to face his hosts.

Bell asked the Hubbards if they knew that a piano could sing back to them. To show what he meant, he stepped on the piano's foot pedal that makes the instrument's strings go slack. Loosened piano strings more easily vibrate than taut ones. Holding down the pedal, Bell loudly sang a single, steady musical note near the strings. As he'd promised, the piano sang back the exact same note. Just like striking a piano key! The trick was caused by resonance, similar to the tuning forks in Bell's earlier experiments. The family was entertained by the demonstration. Quite impressive! But Mr. Hubbard wanted to know if the trick had any practical use. Bell answered yes. In fact, he explained, the same resonance principle of the piano trick could improve the telegraph system.

That caught Mr. Hubbard's attention. A telegraph works by interrupting an electric current connected to a buzzer or other so-called **sounder**. Each short or long buzz makes up a code tapped by the operator when the circuit is complete. The operator on the other end listens to the pattern of buzzes to receive the message. Only one telegraph message at a time could travel over a telegraph wire. Bell figured that more than one message could share a telegraph wire if the buzzes sounded different, for instance if one message had a high pitch and another a low pitch. Different senders and operators on each end of the wire could listen for their specific pitch of buzzes.

Now Hubbard was excited. He realized that his guest was talking about a multiple

The Telegraph

The telegraph was an instrument that sent messages using an electric current over wires. An operator sent a telegram message by tapping on a switch, or key, that opened and closed an electric circuit. The message was made up of a pattern of shorter and longer bursts of current, known as Morse code. The code represented individual letters of the alphabet. An operator on the receiving end decoded the long and short clicking or buzzing made by a sounder into letters that made up a written message.

Samuel Morse invented the first practical telegraph in 1837. By the 1850s, it had become an important way to communicate news and information, and keep track of trains. By the 1860s, most cities had telegraph offices, and telegraph wires were strung across the

The telegraph operators' room at the telegraph exchange in Paris.
Wikimedia Commons

country. Both the Union and Confederate armies communicated via telegraph during the American Civil War.

At first, there were many telegraph companies, each with its own lines of wire and message offices. But many were unreliable and failed. By 1866, most of the United States was covered by the Western Union Telegraph Company. Western Union's **monopoly** helped improve the chances that a message would actually get from one place to another. But sending a telegraph was still a time-consuming chore. The sender had to go to an office, give an operator the message, and wait for it to be sent. And since only one telegraph message could travel along a wire at a time, it could be a long wait. Needless to say, Western Union was desperate to find a way to send multiple messages at once. After all, people paid per message, so the more messages sent, the more money made!

A Civil War–era telegraph key and sounder. Courtesy John Schanlaub

(message) telegraph—a telegraph system that could send and receive multiple messages at once. This was something inventors had been desperately trying to build for years. And his daughter's professor was one of them.

Bell had started thinking about a multiple telegraph after reading a newspaper article that told of the many failures to invent a working one. He realized that the experiments he'd done with electricity and tuning forks could be put to use inventing a telegraph that sent multiple messages. He called his idea for a multiple telegraph a "**harmonic** telegraph." It used differently pitched messages, similar to how chords on a piano play multiple notes at once. Tuning forks of various pitches would send out the messages across a telegraph wire simultaneously. Tuning forks on the receiving end of the wire would pick up the messages sent in their same pitch for the operators to decode. At least that was the idea.

Hubbard listened carefully while Bell explained his harmonic telegraph. Hubbard knew how valuable and useful a multiple telegraph would be. Sending more than one message at a time would make communicating by telegraph faster—and cheaper. It was surely the next big thing in communication technology. How amazing that the man to invent it might be right here in his home!

Mr. Hubbard was a man who knew an opportunity when he saw one. He immediately

offered to fund Bell's experiments. In exchange for his money, Hubbard would share in the invention's profits. Another wealthy parent of a student, Thomas Sanders, had already made Bell the same offer. The men eventually agreed to a three-way partnership. Thomas Sanders and Gardiner Greene Hubbard would pay the inventor's expenses, and the profits of any successes would be split three ways. The Bell Patent Association was born.

Many of Western Union's telegram messengers were boys and young men. National Archives, 306621

KNOW THE CODE

Telegraph messages, or telegrams, arrived in a code of short and long sounds. The man who first patented a telegraph, Samuel Morse, invented the code. That's why it's called Morse code. Hardly anyone sends telegrams these days, but Morse code is still used by many people: anyone needing to communicate using only weak radio signals, like amateur, or ham, radio operators or people who work in aviation and navigation. Emergency response workers learn International Morse Code, too.

The dots and dashes of Morse code don't have to be short and long buzzing sounds—or sounds at all. Any tapping can work. Think of someone trapped in a mine or underneath earthquake rubble tapping out a message by clanging on a pipe. Morse code signals can be transmitted with light, too. The US Navy and Coast Guard use lamps instead of sounds to communicate with Morse code. Even a mirror reflecting a beam of sunlight can work to send the distress call. Morse code is all about timing. The time it takes to signal one dash is equal to the time of three dots. So, for example, a beam of light that's a dash needs to be turned on three times as long as a dot.

Put your imagination to work! How could you send a secret message to a friend using International Morse Code? A flashlight or mirror, foot taps or door slams, or even a recording of sound or light? Send messages back and forth in different ways to find out which medium works for you.

INTERNATIONAL MORSE CODE

The rules:

- One dash equals three dots of time.
- The space between the codes in a letter is equal to a dot of time.
- The space between different letters is equal to three dots of time.
- The space between words is equal to seven dots of time.

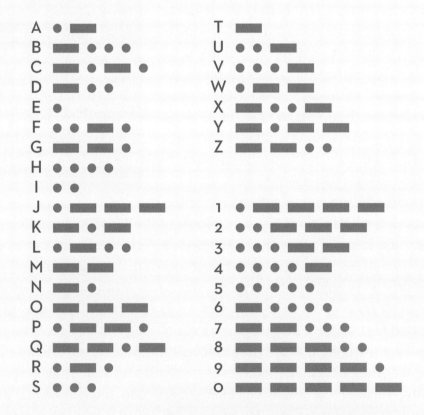

DAYDREAMS OF A SPEAKING TELEGRAPH

BELL THOUGHT his harmonic telegraph idea was good. If it was successful, he'd be a rich and famous inventor. But a multiple telegraph wasn't what he really wanted to work on. Whether telegraph messages were sent one at a time or ten at a time, they were still a code of beeps or clicks that had to be translated by an operator. Wouldn't it be better to send spoken-word messages instead? Think how much faster it would be!

What he really wanted to invent was a "speaking telegraph," a device that would come to be called the telephone. But how could a telegraph wire carry voice sounds? The idea for it came to him during summer break in 1874 after he arrived at his parents' Brantford home. The vacationing university professor soon found himself resting in a familiar spot, an overlook above the Grand River he called his dreaming place.

Bell watched the river roll by and daydreamed. His thoughts wandered from the piano parlor trick to experimenting with electricity. Then his mind bounced from his deaf students to the ear phonautograph he'd made. The sound wave tracings made by the phonautograph looked like smooth, snaking lines. The tracings had an unbroken, **undulating**, up-and-down pattern like an ocean wave. The

Bell's dreaming place overlooking the Grand River, as it looks today. Courtesy Harry Zilber

phonautograms' wavelike patterns proved to Bell that a telegraph could never carry the human voice. Why not? The clicking or buzzing sounds that make up telegraph code are created by interrupting the flow of electricity. The electric current is stopped and started, stopped and started, again and again. Voiced words are different. They flow in unbroken, undulating waves, like the patterns on the phonautograms. A speaking telegraph would have to work in another way.

Bell also knew that as sound waves travel, the pockets of air they pass through squeeze and expand. This is what causes vibrations. The phonautograph he'd made with the real human ear scratched ink off glass. It didn't have a motor or battery. The eardrum vibrating caused the movement. Voice sound waves were strong, powerful enough to make a membrane like an eardrum vibrate, and maybe even powerful enough to control an undulating electric current. And then Bell knew how a telephone could work.

He later wrote that he realized "it would be possible to transmit sounds of any sort if we could only... [vary]... the current exactly like that occurring in the density of air while a given sound is made." And from his experiments with electricity, Bell reasoned that a vibrating magnet could create just the right kind of ebbing and flowing, undulating current. Electricity could carry tones—and therefore the human voice!

But how could a heavy magnet be made to vibrate from just voice sounds? His ear phonautograph held the answer again. Its human eardrum moved the ear bones through vibration. A bigger, thicker membrane could be made to move a metal magnet the same way. "At once the conception of a membrane speaking telephone became complete in my mind." He just had to find out if his idea worked—by building it.

Thomas Watson in the 1880s. Wikimedia Commons

PERFECT PARTNER

Thomas Watson liked his job. He worked at Charles Williams's machine shop making telegraph and fire alarm equipment. Watson was one of the shop's best machinists, and the 20-year-old often did custom work for inventors. A grimy workbench covered in bits of metal, wire, wood, and every tool imaginable were like clay to a potter for Watson. He could create any kind of electric device a customer asked for. "I made stubborn metal do my will and take the shape necessary to enable it to do its allotted work," Watson recalled.

One day in 1874, Watson looked up from his workbench to see an unknown gentleman rushing through the office and into the shop. *That's odd*, thought Watson. Customers were supposed to first talk to someone in the office, not just walk into the shop. Watson remembered the visitor as "a tall, slender, quick-motioned young man with a pale face, black side-whiskers and drooping mustache, big nose and high, sloping forehead crowned with bushy jet-black hair."

The impatient customer was 27-year-old Alexander Graham Bell. The Boston University professor walked right up to Watson and began quizzing him about different devices. Bell knew that he needed the help of a skilled craftsman if he was ever going to build a working invention. "I... was always clumsy in the

Thomas A. Watson

Thomas Augustus Watson was born in Salem, Massachusetts. His father ran a livery stable, a place that rented out horses and carriages. Watson wasn't much for classroom work and left school at age 14. He went from one job to another, looking for work he enjoyed. At 18, he started working at a machine shop in Boston. He not only liked the work but also had a talent for machinery. He quickly became very good at making electric machines and devices for the shop's customers, including inventors like Alexander Graham Bell.

Helping Bell invent the telephone made Watson a wealthy man. He went on to start a successful shipbuilding business that grew into the largest in the United States. Never one to stop learning, he also studied geology and paleontology and had a group of fossil snails named for him. Later in life, he turned to acting and playwriting. He also lectured about the telephone and wrote his autobiography, titled *Exploring Life*, which was published in 1926.

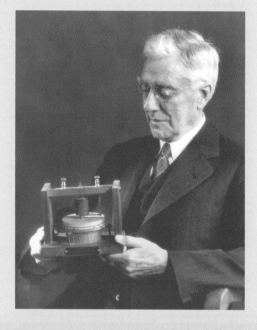

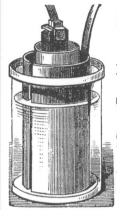

Thomas Watson started working at Charles Williams's shop in 1871. Wikimedia Commons

LEFT: Thomas Watson in 1931.
Library of Congress, LC-USZ62-59660

use of my hands and inefficient where tools were concerned," Bell wrote. Watson was just the help he needed.

Watson soon started working with Bell on his inventions, and the men became close friends, too. "No finer influence than Graham Bell ever came into my life," Watson wrote. The two men's partnership would become one of the most memorable in the history of inventions.

Bell now had mechanical help from Watson and financial help from the Bell Patent Association. A **patent** is an official government document that allows only the inventor to make, use, or sell that particular invention. A patent protects an inventor's idea from being stolen.

The pressure was turned up on Bell to quickly invent and patent his multiple

PIE TIN TELEGRAPH

You'll Need

- Aluminum pie tin
- Ruler
- Scissors
- Wire strippers
- D alkaline battery
- Duct tape
- Platform (use an old magazine or a piece of thick cardboard)
- Rubber bands
- Pen or pencil
- 1½-volt buzzer with lead wires (available at hobby and electronics stores)
- 10-inch (25-cm) length of insulated copper wire
- 2 metal thumbtacks

1. Make a battery holder: Cut a 5-by-1-inch (12½-by-2½-cm) rectangle out of the pie tin. Set the battery lengthwise on the tin strip and fold up the ends to make a kind of cradle.

2. Set aside the battery and tape down the middle of the battery holder to the platform. Slip the battery back in the holder and use a rubber band to hold the metal tightly against both ends of the battery, as shown.

3. Write + on the platform near the positive end of the battery. That's the end with the raised contact bump. Write – on the platform near the other, negative, end of the battery. Pull back the side of the battery holder, place the end of the red buzzer wire onto the positive contact of the battery, and tape it on. Make sure the tape holds the wire to the contact, as shown.

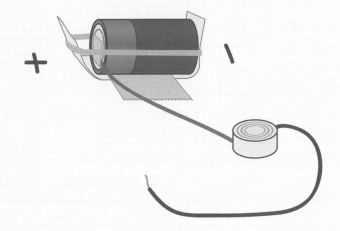

4. Ask an adult to help you use the wire strippers to remove the insulation off an inch (2½ cm) of both ends of the length of wire.

5. Pull back the other side of the battery holder, place one end of the insulated wire onto the negative contact of the battery, and tape it on, too.

6. Cut out a 2-by-1-inch (5-by-2½-cm) rectangle from the pie tin and set it on the platform. Wrap the other end of the insulated wire around a metal thumbtack; then push the thumbtack through the tin and into the platform, as shown. Fold over the tin so it covers the thumbtack and tape one end down to secure it.

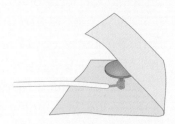

7. Cut out a ½-inch-wide (1¼-cm) strip of tin that includes the crimped edge, as shown.

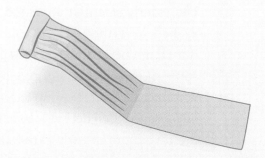

8. Wrap the end of the buzzer's black wire around a thumbtack and push it through the flat end of the tin piece from step 7. Before folding the tin over the thumbtack and securing it in place, move it around so that the crimped part of the tin hovers over the tin-wrapped first thumbtack, as shown.

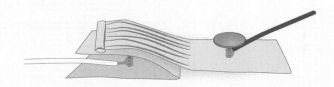

9. Try out your telegraph! Tap down on the hovering end of the crimped tin so it touches the tin-wrapped thumbtack. This completes the circuit. Buzzzzz!

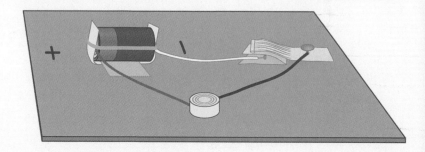

harmonic telegraph idea. Time was running out; other inventors were working on their own multiple telegraph designs. If the competition got its device working and patented first, the Bell Patent Association would get no profit from its investment in Professor Bell.

PRESSURE AND ADVICE

BELL AND Watson toiled at the harmonic multiple telegraph in an attic workshop in Boston all that winter. Bell was under a lot of pressure to beat the competition, but he never stopped thinking about his idea for a speaking telegraph, the telephone. It was the invention that inspired him. No one would want a crude dot-and-dash code telegraph once voices could travel along wires, he reasoned. But Bell's harmonic telegraph was what the Bell Patent Association was backing him to invent. The race to invent and patent a multiple telegraph must be won first.

By late winter of 1875, Watson and Bell had made progress. Hubbard and Sanders sent their inventor off to file patents on the harmonic telegraph technologies. In March 1875, Bell boarded a train for Washington, DC, and the US Patent Office. While in the nation's capital, he visited a famous scientist. Joseph Henry of the Smithsonian Institution had made many discoveries about electricity and **electromagnetism**. He'd also worked on telegraph technology. Henry's ideas had helped Samuel Morse invent the telegraph. Perhaps Henry would be interested in his inventions, Bell thought.

The Smithsonian Institution sits halfway between the Washington Monument and the Capitol Building in Washington, DC. Bell was likely a bit nervous meeting the important scientist in such an impressive setting. Henry didn't seem that pleased to meet Bell either. The elderly scientist appeared uninterested as Bell described his harmonic telegraph. But Henry perked up when Bell showed him some of the electric equipment that he and Watson had built. Feeling more relaxed and encouraged, Bell decided to share his idea for the invention he truly cared about. He told Henry about the telephone.

····· The Smithsonian Institution ·····

In 1829, British scientist James Smithson left his fortune to the US government. He gave the money to create a place for the "increase and diffusion of knowledge among men." Congress set up the Smithsonian Institution in 1846 in Washington, DC, and appointed the most revered American scientist of the time, physicist Joseph Henry, its first director.

Today the Smithsonian Institution is a nonprofit organization of scientific, educational, and cultural interests. It includes more than a dozen museums, the National Zoo, and *Smithsonian* magazine.

Basic Electric Know-How

Electricity is a kind of energy created by atoms gaining and losing electrons. When electrons move, they carry electric energy with them. This is electric current.

An electric current needs a circuit, or pathway, in order to flow. For a circuit to work, it has to be a closed loop.

Circuits are made by connecting components with something that passes along, or conducts, electricity. Metal, including copper wire, easily conducts electricity.

A flashlight circuit has a bulb, battery, and switch in a loop. The switch turns off the flashlight by breaking the circuit.

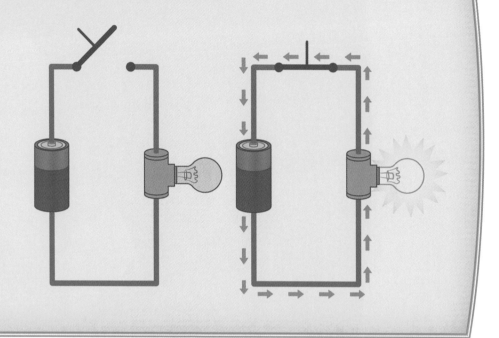

After explaining to Henry how a device might be able to carry voices with electricity, Bell asked the scientist for advice: Should he publish his idea now and leave the inventing to others? Henry had himself missed out on a number of inventions by not patenting his own ideas early enough. Perhaps he didn't want the young inventor to repeat his own mistake. "[Henry] said he thought it was 'the germ of a great invention' and advised me to work at it myself," Bell wrote in a letter to his parents. When Bell complained to Henry that he didn't have the electric know-how to invent it, the 77-year-old physicist scolded, "Get it!" Bell wrote his parents, "I cannot tell you how much these two words have encouraged me." Bell would later admit, "But for Joseph Henry, I would never have gone ahead with the telephone."

This replica of Bell's attic laboratory was built to look exactly like the inventor's October 1875 workshop.
Library of Congress, LCCN2011630417

"Mr. Watson—Come Here"

4

Alexander Graham Bell arrived home from Washington, DC, eager to get back to his experiments. Joseph Henry's enthusiasm for his telephone idea had reenergized Bell. Surely he was onto something big! He shared his excitement in a letter to his parents. "Every moment of my time is devoted to study of electricity and to experiments," he wrote in the spring of 1875. "I think the transmission of the human voice is much more nearly at hand than I supposed."

Back in his Boston laboratory, Bell and Watson toiled with the unfinished harmonic telegraph. Bell really wanted to work on the telephone. He shared his frustrations with his friend and work partner. "If I can get a mechanism which makes a current of electricity vary in its intensity, as the air varies in density when a sound is passing through it, I can telegraph any sound, even the sound of speech," Watson remembered him explaining. Bell was convinced that the telephone would be a much more important invention than the harmonic telegraph. Who cared if a harmonic telegraph could send three messages—or a dozen—at once?

Mabel Gardiner Hubbard was a poised, well-educated woman. Library of Congress, LC-G9-Z1-156,508-A

Any dot-and-dash telegraph would be unwanted once voices could travel over wires. At least that's what Bell believed.

Gardiner Greene Hubbard disagreed. The wealthy lawyer, and Bell's source of money, thought the telephone was too futuristic. It was like inventing a train before the steam engine, he thought. Hubbard wanted a sure bet, an invention guaranteed to make money. What if Bell built a working telephone and no one wanted to buy it? He risked losing the money he'd invested. But not with the multiple telegraph. People already wanted to buy them! Inventing the first one would earn them all a lot of money.

The choice was obvious. Hubbard demanded that Bell not work on any sort of talking-by-wire invention. He forced Bell to set aside his telephone dream for now. The trouble between Bell and Hubbard wasn't going away anytime soon. In fact, it was about to get a lot worse—and much more complicated. Bell wanted to marry the boss's daughter.

LOVE AND IN-LAWS

AFTER YEARS spent as Mabel Hubbard's teacher and dinner guest—and an employee of her father's—Bell had fallen in love with her. Alexander and Mabel's tutoring sessions had turned into long, ongoing conversations. They discussed art, music, books, and politics.

Alexander found 17-year-old Mabel to be intelligent and charming, as well as warm and caring.

Mabel didn't know of Alexander's love for her. The proper way to start a courtship in those days was by contacting the parents. A young gentleman was expected to seek permission before courting, or dating, a young woman. Alexander did just that. In a letter to the Hubbards, he wrote, "I have discovered that my interest in my dear pupil… has ripened into a far deeper feeling." The 28-year-old Alexander requested to court Mabel. The Hubbards did not approve. They asked him to keep his feelings secret from Mabel, at least for the next year. Once she was 18, she'd be older and able to decide for herself about a suitor.

Alexander suffered in silence that summer but kept his word to his beloved's parents. But his secret escaped through a gossiping cousin who told Mabel. In a string of letters, Alexander risked opening his heart to her. He wrote to her of "my wish to make you my wife—if you would let me try to win your love." She answered honestly, telling him that she respected him greatly as her tutor. But the teenager admitted that she did not love him—nor was she even sure what love was yet. Alexander was actually encouraged by her answer! *At least she didn't reject me completely*, he thought. He kept writing her, and Mabel eventually agreed to a courtship.

How Mabel Met Alexander

Mabel Hubbard wasn't born deaf. Her hearing was fine until she caught a bad case of **scarlet fever** when she was five. High fevers in small children can damage the nerves involved in sensing sound. Mabel had learned to talk years before losing her hearing. After the fever left her deaf, she continued to speak.

But over the years of silence, her speech grew less clear. Her words muddied, and over time people found her harder to understand. It was especially difficult for her when meeting strangers. They often ignored her after they found out she was deaf. But Mabel could read lips—in several languages. She painfully understood every rude comment made about her. The dark-eyed teenager with long hair didn't want their pity. She wanted to be treated as an equal.

When Mabel met her new tutor, she was doubtful that Professor Bell could help her speak. Her wealthy parents had already hired tutors for her in America and Europe, but none had really helped her improve her speech. When they met in 1873, 15-year-old Mabel wasn't very impressed with Alexander Graham Bell. The wealthy, European-educated teenager complained in her diary that "he dressed badly and carelessly in an old-fashioned suit." But Professor Bell's teaching soon won Mabel's respect. A few months later, just after she turned 16, she wrote her mother that her speech was already greatly improved.

Alexander, on the other hand, was immediately impressed with Mabel. She was intelligent, interested in the world around her, and a hardworking student. He also thought her poised and strikingly beautiful.

Mabel had normal hearing when this portrait of her was taken around age three. Library of Congress, LC-USZ6-2007

Now that he had marriage on his mind, Bell realized he needed to earn more money. Mabel would more likely accept his proposal if he could provide for a family, he thought. His tutoring business had suffered from all the time he'd spent working on the harmonic telegraph. Teaching was how he earned a living, after all.

But when Bell traded some of his time working on the harmonic telegraph for paid tutoring sessions of Visible Speech, Gardiner Greene Hubbard was furious. The competition was going to beat them to the invention, he said, and all because of Bell's lack of focus. The criticism wasn't coming just from his employer but also from the man Alexander hoped would one day be his father-in-law. Hubbard demanded that Bell make a decision: either give up his career teaching the deaf, or give up Mabel and inventing. The choice was Bell's.

Heat and Pressure

High temperatures didn't agree with Bell. The gentleman Scot preferred cool weather more appropriate to his wool suits. The heat gave him headaches and made him irritable. June 2, 1875, was one such hot, frustrating day. The attic workshop above the machine shop was sweltering. Bell and Watson had been sweating it out all day there, testing the harmonic telegraph invention, and the device wasn't cooperating. "In spite of Bell's hard study on his telegraph invention… we couldn't make it work rightly," wrote Watson.

The men were trying to get their harmonic telegraph to send three telegraph messages at the same time by making all three electric signals a different pitch. Bell had abandoned the idea of using tuning forks to shuttle the precise pitches. Now vibrating reeds made of thin strips of steel sang out the harmonic telegraph's tones. Bell and Watson were painstakingly adjusting the screws that held the metal reeds that steamy June evening. Then something quite strange happened.

Watson was in the room with the **transmitters**, the equipment for sending messages. Bell was in another room with the **receivers**, the equipment that received the sent messages. At least that's what the receivers were supposed to do. As he'd done time and again, Watson tried to send messages to Bell in the next room, but they weren't going through. The small metal reeds were so fussy! Each one had to be screwed down just right to keep vibrating—not too tight or too loose. The men kept at it, trying again to send messages. When one of the transmitter reeds stopped vibrating again, Watson grabbed a screwdriver. "I began to readjust the screw while continuing to pluck the reed, when I was startled by a loud shout from Bell," wrote Watson. Bell came rushing from the other room, asking Watson what he had done.

Bell's harmonic telegraph had a vibrating reed made of a metal strip and a barrel-shaped electromagnet below it. Museums Victoria, http://collections.museumvictoria.com.au/items/411376

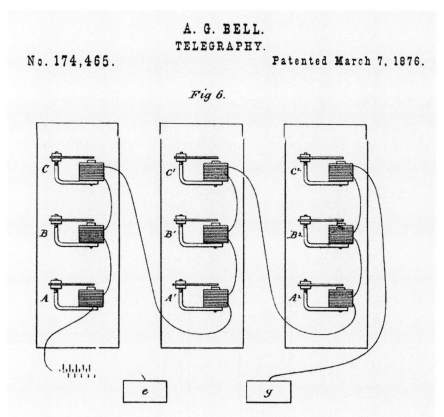

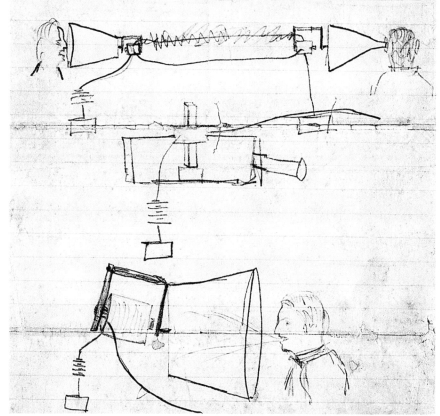

The reed on Bell's receiver end had vibrated with Watson's plucking, singing out twangs of sound. Bell's musical ear recognized the sound as more than a single telegraph tone. Watson had been both plucking and adjusting the vibrating steel-strip reed with a screwdriver—unknowingly causing the reed to vary its vibrations and therefore its tone, like tuning a guitar. The surprising part was that by changing the sound vibrations, Watson had also varied the electric current. And the reed on the receiver end had reproduced the very same variation in current as sound. That's what the sound coming from Bell's receiver was. The changing sound had been shuttled over the wires, just as Bell had dreamed the summer before! The electric current was undulating, just like sound waves, creating a stream of sound-shaped electricity. The current was never stopped and restarted, like in a telegraph; it just varied. If electricity could transmit the complex sound he'd just heard,

LEFT: Bell's design for a harmonic telegraph was part of his famous patent. National Archives, 6120306

ABOVE: A sketch by Bell of his ideas for the first telephone. The top drawing shows the transmitter (mouthpiece) on the left and the receiver (earpiece) on the right. The lower sketch is a more detailed drawing of how a person would speak into the transmitter. Library of Congress, 27300105

GET IN TUNE

Alexander Graham Bell knew a telephone needed to be able to turn sound waves into an undulating wave of electricity. Then voice sounds could be transmitted over wire. But how? Electric resistance, or how easily the current flows, was the answer. A current with changing electric resistance—but never completely interrupted—could carry the changing tones of speech.

Re-create an experiment similar to one of Bell's to see how an electric circuit can carry a sound's frequency. The tuning fork's vibrations change the resistance of the current flowing between the vinegar and the tuning fork. The changed resistance causes the current reaching the speaker to fluctuate at the same frequency (or pitch) as the tuning fork.

Adult supervision required

You'll Need

- Insulated copper wire, about 5 feet (2 m)
- Wire strippers
- Scissors
- 6-volt battery (the kind that goes into a camping lantern or big flashlight)
- Small speaker scavenged from old telephone receiver, radio, etc. (needs to have two lead wires attached to it)
- Tuning fork (any tone, musical or scientific)
- Metal measuring cup with handle
- White vinegar (5%)

1. Ask an adult to help you cut the wire in half. Set aside one half as piece B. Divide the other half into two shorter pieces, C and A. Have an adult help you use wire strippers to remove the last inch (2½ cm) of insulation from both ends of all three wire pieces.

A   B   C

2. Make a complete circuit with the battery, speaker, tuning fork, and cup. Wire A connects one terminal of the battery to one of the speaker wires. Wire B connects the other speaker wire to the handle end of the tuning fork. Wire C connects the second battery terminal to the cup handle. Twist the wires at each connection point to close the circuit.

3. Check the circuit by touching the tuning fork to the metal cup. Static-like noise should come through the speaker. If it's not working, recheck your connections.

4. Fill the metal cup three-quarters full with vinegar.

5. Practice making the tuning fork sing. Give it a good rap on the table, holding onto the handle but without touching the wire.

6. Lean your ear close to the speaker. Then strike the tuning fork and quickly lower it toward the vinegar. Keep the prongs as parallel as you can to the surface of the vinegar and dip one prong into the liquid.

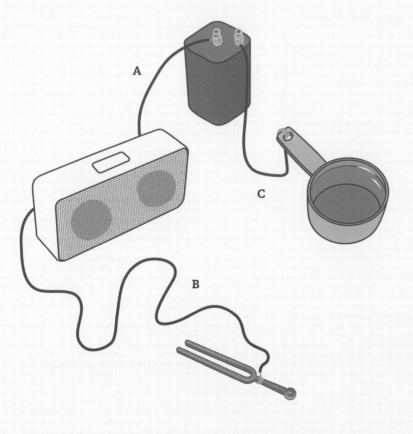

7. Repeat step 6 until you hear a tone coming through the speaker.

8. Repeat step 6, but keep the prongs out of the vinegar. Does the tone still come through? What if both prongs are submerged?

it could transmit the human voice. Bell knew it would work. "The speaking telephone was born at that moment," wrote Watson. Before the long, hot night was over, Bell had sketched out a design for the first telephone.

········ Bell's Electromagnetism ········

Bell's early telephone designs grew out of his work on a harmonic telegraph. Both instruments depended on the principles of electromagnetism. Electromagnetism is the relationship between electricity and magnetism—how one affects the other. An electric current can make a magnetic field, and a magnetic field can produce an electric current. When electric current flows through wire, the electricity creates a magnetic field. If that magnetic field is increased, so is the flow of electric current, because one affects the other.

An electromagnet is a chunk of iron wrapped in wire. When electricity flows through the wire, the electromagnet becomes magnetized. It stops being a magnet when the electric current stops. The amount of current changes the strength of an electromagnet. Turning up the juice on an electromagnet makes it more powerful.

In early telephone designs, transmitters (the piece you speak into) contained an electromagnet. The current flowing through the telephone's electromagnet varied in strength with the sound waves. A voice vibrated air, creating sound waves that vibrated the **diaphragm** of the telephone transmitter. When the iron in the diaphragm vibrated near the pole of the electromagnet, the magnetic field changed, causing the current in the electromagnet wire to change in the same way. Bell called this undulating current. This changing magnetic field created a current that was part of a circuit leading to the receiver. The reverse happened at the receiver, and the sounds were re-created.

BACKING DOWN AND GEARING UP

THE ACCIDENTAL discovery that June was a turning point for Bell. He felt confident that his idea would make a working telephone—his dream invention. But everything wasn't perfect in his world. He was upset, angry, and offended by what Gardiner Greene Hubbard had said. Asking him to choose between tutoring and Mabel was unfair—and wrong! Bell considered his lifework to be teaching the deaf to speak. And Visible Speech was part of his family heritage. He wouldn't give that up to invent a better telegraph or to please the father of the woman he loved.

Bell angrily wrote in a letter to Mabel's father, "If she does not come to love me well enough to accept me whatever my profession or business may be—I do not want her at all! I do not want a half-love, nor do I want her to marry my profession!" Mabel herself put the conflict forever to rest on November 25, 1875. It was her 18th birthday, Thanksgiving Day, and the day she agreed to marry an astonished Alexander. He had won her heart! "I am afraid to go to sleep lest I should find it all a dream," he wrote her that night. "So I shall lie awake and think of you."

Adding to Bell's bliss was Gardiner Greene Hubbard's complete change of mind about working on the telephone. Now that Bell felt he was so near to inventing the "speaking telegraph," Hubbard backed off on the harmonic telegraph. Perhaps the businessman finally saw the telephone's potential. Maybe the gossip about other inventors working on similar inventions convinced him that the telephone was the real race to win. Whatever the reason, Hubbard now pushed Bell to invent a working telephone and patent the device.

The effort went into high gear. Rumors swirled that other inventors, including an engineer named Elisha Gray, were close to success. Hubbard and the other Bell Patent Associates needed to be first. There's no second place in the inventing world. You either get the patent or you don't. The competition was on their heels.

A First Try

Watson turned the design that Bell had sketched on June 2 into a working telephone before the month was over. The very first telephone was a revamped harmonic telegraph transmitter of sorts. It still had a metal strip that contacted the electromagnet to send signals. But the steel strip was connected by a thin cork to a vibrating diaphragm made of a membrane tightly stretched over a wide, stout wooden tube, like a drumhead. This was the mouthpiece. When Bell or Watson spoke into the back of the drumlike mouthpiece, sound waves traveled toward the diaphragm and caused it to vibrate. The vibrations passed into a spring, which vibrated over one end of an electromagnet. The electromagnet created an electric current that transmitted the voice sounds to a receiver. The receiver

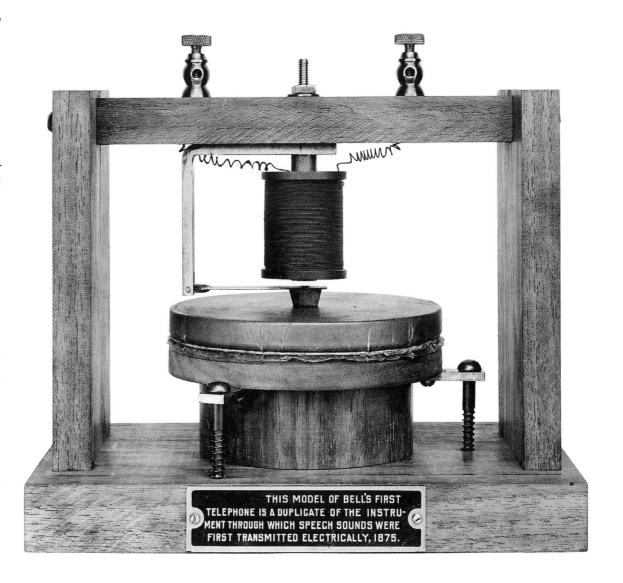

The first telephone built by Bell and Watson in late 1875. The mouthpiece was the underside hole in the labeled platform, below the drum. To use it, you'd turn it on its side and speak into that hole. Transmitted words were unclear, but it worked.

Library of Congress, LC-DIG-det-4a27893

THIS MODEL OF BELL'S FIRST TELEPHONE IS A DUPLICATE OF THE INSTRUMENT THROUGH WHICH SPEECH SOUNDS WERE FIRST TRANSMITTED ELECTRICALLY, 1875.

was pretty much the same as the one for the harmonic telegraph. It used a vibrating steel strip to reproduce the sounds of the words spoken. The telephone worked, but the sounds were rough and garbled and weren't understandable as words.

The telephone invention wasn't ready for store shelves yet. Still, Bell had worked out the basic principles and design. They were making progress—enough to draw unwanted attention. The attic workshop above where Watson worked was too public. Lots of nosy inventors came through Williams's machine shop. Deciding it was too risky to work on the telephone there, Bell moved into a different Boston boardinghouse in January 1876. He used one of its rooms as a private workshop.

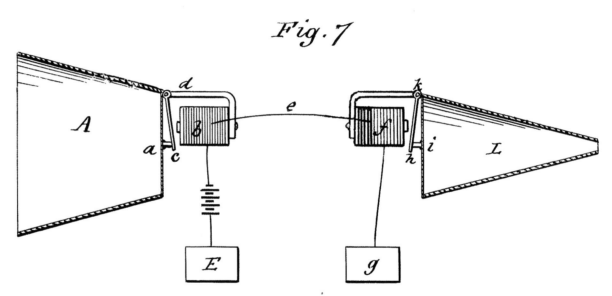

Fig. 7

This simple diagram illustrates how the telephone works in Bell's 1876 patent. His explanation reads: "Another mode is shown in Fig. 7, whereby motions can be imparted to the armature by the human voice or by means of a musical instrument. The armature *c*, Fig. 7, is fastened loosely by one extremity to the uncovered leg *d* of the electro-magnet *b*, and its other extremity is attached to the centre of a stretched membrane, *a*. A cone, *A*, is used to converge sound-vibrations upon the membrane. When a sound is uttered in the cone the membrane *a* is set in vibration, the armature *c* is forced to partake of the motion, and thus electric undulations are created upon the circuit *E-b-e-f-g*. These undulations are similar in sound to the air vibrations caused by the sound—that is, they are represented graphically by similar curves. The undulatory current passing through the electro-magnet *f* influences its armature *h* to copy the motions of the armature *c*. A similar sound to that uttered into *A* is then heard to proceed from *L*." National Archives, 302052

Elisha Gray

Elisha Gray was an American inventor based in Chicago who competed with Alexander Graham Bell on the multiple telegraph and telephone. In fact, Elisha Gray later teamed up with the Western Union Telegraph Company against Bell in a court battle over the telephone's patent.

Some consider Gray the true inventor of the telephone because the device he described in his **patent caveat** would have likely worked. In contrast, the magnetoelectric telephone design in Bell's patent was somewhat different from the liquid transmitter model he went on to develop.

An illustrated portrait of Elisha Gray from around 1878.
Wikimedia Commons

Gray became a wealthy man thanks to his many telegraphic and electric inventions. He held about 70 patents and was a respected professor of electricity at Oberlin College. But he was bitter about coming in second in the telephone race. It was understandably a sore point for the rest of his life. After Gray died, a note he'd written was found that read, "The history of the telephone will never be fully written.... It is partly hidden away... and partly lying on the hearts and consciences of a few whose lips are sealed—some in death and others by a golden clasp whose grip is even tighter."

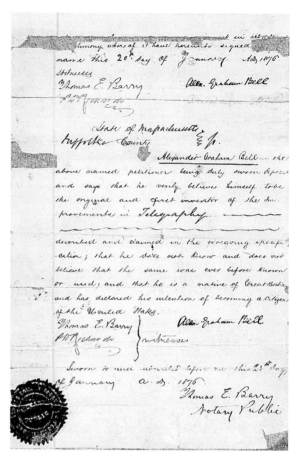

US Patent No. 174,465: Improvements in Telegraphy. National Archives, 595437

That winter, Bell wrote up an explanation of his so-called magnetoelectric membrane telephone, along with labeled diagrams. It became the patent paperwork filed by the Bell Patent Association on February 14, 1876—not a moment too soon! Just a few hours later that same day, rival inventor Elisha Gray filed a patent caveat. A patent caveat was a legal document telling other inventors that a patent application was in the works. It was a way to claim an invention in progress. (The US Patent Office stopped allowing caveats in 1910.)

ELECTROMAGNET MAGIC

Discover how electric and magnetic fields relate to each other in this activity.

Adult supervision required

You'll Need

- Insulated copper wire
- Screwdriver with plastic or wood handle
- Wire strippers
- Strong tape (duct or electric)
- 9-volt battery
- Metal paper clips

1. Tightly wind the wire around the screwdriver's metal shaft, beginning where the shaft connects to the handle to an inch (2½ cm) or so from the tip. Completely cover most of the screwdriver shaft with wire, leaving a 4-inch (10-cm) tail of wire on both ends.

2. Use tape to snugly hold the first and last coils in place on the screwdriver shaft. The wire tails need to remain free, as shown.

3. Ask an adult to help you use wire strippers to remove the insulation from that last inch (2½ cm) of each wire tail.

4. Connect the wires to the battery. Wrap one stripped end of a wire tail around a terminal and then repeat with the other wire tail. Use strong tape to secure them.

5. Your electromagnet is ready. Hold it by the handle and use the tip of the screwdriver to pick up the metal paper clips or other small objects that contain iron. What happens to the paperclips when you disconnect a terminal of the battery?

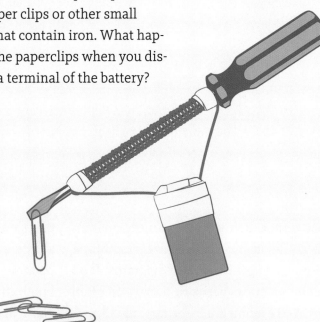

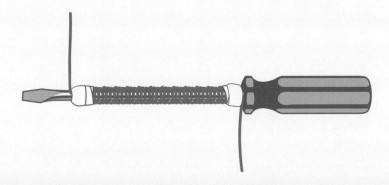

Gray's patent caveat warned that he would soon be filing a patent for a device to electrically transmit speech, claiming he was working on an electric speaking telephone. Luckily for Bell, his detailed and thorough patent application got there first. US Patent No. 174,465 was granted on March 7, 1876. No one had yet made a call by telephone, but it would become one of the most profitable inventions in history.

THE FIRST TELEPHONE MESSAGE

BACK FROM the Patent Office in Washington, DC, Bell quickly got down to business. His telephone was protected by a patent. Now all that was left to do was to make it work. On the first day back in the workshop, Bell decided to try something different. He abandoned the steel strip and big drumlike mouthpiece and began experimenting with a new kind of transmitter. This one used liquid to help transfer voice vibrations into electric signals. He quickly figured out that watered-down battery acid was the best liquid to use; it made the sound much louder.

Bell and Watson hooked up the new liquid transmitter and tried it out. When Watson spoke into the top of the transmitter cone, his voice vibrated a membrane. A needle attached to the shaking membrane then bobbed up

How the Liquid Transmitter Telephone Works

1. Speaking into the transmitter's cone creates sound waves.

2. Sound waves vibrate the membrane stretched across the bottom of the cone.

3. The vibrations cause a metal needle attached to the center of the membrane to move up and down in a cup of watered-down acid.

4. When the needle moves closer to the wire at the bottom of the cup, there's less resistance to the flow of electricity between the needle and wire. Less resistance means the electric current increases. The current weakens from an increase in electric resistance when the needle moves away from the wire.

5. The variations in electric resistance create a current with an up-and-down flow. This wavelike, undulating current travels along a wire to the receiver. The receiver's metal reed vibrates with the undulating current, reproducing the same variations in electric resistance that create imitated speech sounds.

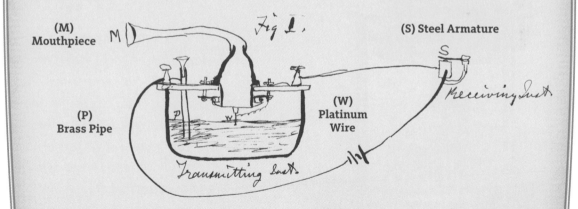

This sketch from a page of Bell's personal notebook is dated March 10, 1876, the day of the first successful telephone call. The notes below the sketch begin, "The improved instrument shown in Fig.1 was constructed this morning and tried this evening."
Library of Congress, 25300201

and down in the liquid. The voice vibrations traveled from the transmitter to a wire that led to a metal reed in the receiver. "When Mr. Watson talked into the box an indistinct mumbling was heard at [the receiver]," Bell noted on March 9, 1876. The inventor could hear his assistant speaking. But the telephone's sound still wasn't clear enough to make out specific words.

The next morning, March 10, Watson made a new liquid transmitter. "Mr. Watson was stationed in one room with the Receiving Instrument. He pressed one ear closely against [the receiver] and closed his other ear with his hand," Bell wrote in his lab notebook. "The Transmitting Instrument was placed in another room and the door of both rooms were closed." Watson waited in Bell's bedroom with the telephone's steel reed receiver up against his ear. Bell was in a separate room with the new liquid transmitter. "I then shouted into [the mouthpiece] the following sentence: 'Mr. Watson—Come here—I want to see you.'"

A stunned Watson rushed into the hallway where Bell was. "To my delight he came and declared that he had heard and understood what I said," wrote Bell. Bell had transmitted the first words by telephone! The men

Bell's liquid transmitter telephone. It was the first telephone to transmit understandable words.
Wikimedia Commons

········ Truth or Legend? ········

Why did Alexander Graham Bell speak those famous words, "Mr. Watson—Come here—I want to see you"? When Watson wrote about the event in his autobiography, he said that Bell sounded alarmed. Watson wrote that he rushed into Bell's room and found that his mentor had spilled battery acid on his clothes.

The acid-spilling accident has become part of the legend of the first telephone call, but did it really happen? Bell made no mention of spilling acid in his own account. Did it not seem important? Or had Bell simply heard strange noises coming through the device and wanted to know what Watson had done?

Watson's account wasn't published until he wrote his autobiography 50 years after the fateful day. Bell had by then passed away. Perhaps acid was spilled or perhaps not. With or without the spill, it was a historic day, well worth remembering.

switched places, and Watson spoke the first telephoned words that Bell would hear: "Mr. Bell, do you understand what I say?"

Later, as the day's importance sunk in, Bell wrote a letter to his father: "Articulate speech was transmitted intelligibly this afternoon. I have constructed a new apparatus operated by the human voice.... This is a great day with me. I feel that I have at last struck the solution of a great problem—and the day is coming when [telephone] wires will be laid on to houses just like water or gas—and friends converse with each other without leaving home." Alexander Graham Bell had invented the telephone. It was time to call the world and let them know.

Alexander Graham Bell around 1876. He was 28 years old when he invented the telephone.
Library of Congress, LC-G9-Z1-14931-A

Visitors came to Machinery Hall in 1876 to see all sorts of new gadgets and inventions, including this wallpaper printer. Library of Congress, LC-USZ62-108122

On the Road and on to New Inventions

5

The United States of America turned 100 years old in 1876. The century-old nation threw itself a birthday party, called the **Centennial** Exhibition. Nearly 10 million people came to Philadelphia, Pennsylvania, to celebrate and see the sights. The exhibition featured art, culture, and foods from the 37 United States, as well as competition among the latest inventions. The centennial event in Philadelphia displayed the day's cutting-edge technologies for judges. Within the huge Machinery Hall full of steam engines, cannons, and printing presses was a small, out-of-the-way exhibit. It displayed items from Massachusetts, including some odd-looking electric equipment. It was Alexander Graham Bell's newest telephone.

As Bell readied his invention for the judges, no one watching would've guessed that the tall, dark-haired inventor was only 29. Any hint of boyishness was long gone in Bell. He hadn't really wanted to compete at the Centennial Exhibition. It was exam time back at Boston University. His students likely needed his help, and he had tests to grade, too. But his fiancée, Mabel Hubbard, talked him into going and

showing off his invention. What wider audience was there than the biggest fair in American history?

One of the judges was the exhibition's most distinguished visitor: Pedro II, emperor of Brazil. On the hot afternoon of June 25, 1876, everyone stared as Emperor Pedro held the telephone receiver up to his ear. Meanwhile, 500 feet (152 m) away, Bell began reciting Shakespeare into a transmitter. A startled Pedro jumped out of his chair and exclaimed

ABOVE: Pedro II was Brazil's last emperor and reigned for nearly 50 years. Wikimedia Commons

LEFT: This portrait of Alexander Graham Bell was painted in 1882.
Library of Congress, LC-USZ62-104275

in astonishment, "I hear, I hear!" The other judges rushed to be the next in line to listen to Bell's voice through the telephone. Loud cheers rose up after each successful test. The crowd around Bell's telephone made such a racket that exhibition police thought the building was on fire! Famed English scientist Sir William Thomson declared it the most wonderful thing he'd seen in America: "Before long, friends will whisper their secrets over the electric wire."

NOVELTY OR NECESSITY?

THE TELEPHONE Bell displayed in Philadelphia was an improvement over the liquid transmitter that had first transmitted understandable speech three months earlier. It had evolved into a two-way speaking and listening device that shuttled speaking voices over telegraph wires at distances of up to 2 miles (3 km). Bell's telephone was a marvel! It thrilled the judges at the Centennial Exhibition. But it wasn't making any money. "Of what use is such an invention?" asked a New York newspaper in late 1876. No one seemed to understand the telephone's value.

The Bell Patent Association was now four men. Thomas Watson had joined Gardiner Greene Hubbard, Alexander Graham Bell, and Thomas Sanders in the group. The men decided to try to earn a profit from their in-

vestment by selling it to Western Union Telegraph Company. The company already had a network of telegraph wires strung across America. Who better to set up a telephone system? Bell's asking price for the telephone's patent was $100,000.

Western Union's president turned down the offer. He declared Bell's telephone to be nothing more than an amusing toy. It

Bell brought more than one kind of telephone to the Centennial Exhibition in 1876, as illustrated in this newspaper article. The top transmitter (left) and receiver (right) was the model Pedro II tried. Wikimedia Commons

was perhaps the worst business decision in American history. "Two years later those same patents could not have been bought for $25 million," wrote Watson. But in 1876, Western Union's rejection left the Bell Patent Association with an unprofitable invention—

Public demonstrations, like the one illustrated here in an 1877 issue of *Scientific American*, proved that the telephone worked across long distances. *Scientific American*, March 31, 1877

just as Gardiner Greene Hubbard had feared. If they wanted to sell telephones to the public, they'd have to do it themselves.

Just like he and his father had done with Visible Speech, Bell arranged public lectures to demonstrate the telephone. Most attendees viewed these events as their evening's entertainment. Audiences were astonished when they heard Watson's voice coming through a box on a stage answering Bell's questions, even though Watson was miles away. "I am the invisible Tom Watson!" the voice from the telephone would exclaim. "Everybody hears me! Nobody sees me!" The two men put on an entertaining show, adding drama and even singing.

Bell and Watson's telephone show was a hit. The upper-class Hubbards were a bit shocked and embarrassed that their daughter's fiancé was amusing audiences with such antics. But they couldn't complain about the results. Little more than a year after the Centennial Exhibition, nearly 800 Bell telephones had been ordered and installed. It was catching on as useful technology for businesses. The telephone was much more than an amusing toy.

In July 1877, Bell, Sanders, Watson, and Hubbard formed the Bell Telephone Company. With his invention finally making money, 30-year-old Alexander could support a wife. He and Mabel married on July 11, 1877.

The inventor's wedding gift to his wife was his entire 30 percent share of the Bell Telephone Company. The gift soon made 19-year-old Mabel Bell a very wealthy woman.

FIT FOR A QUEEN AND A PRESIDENT

THE NEWLYWEDS boarded a steamship in August and headed to Great Britain. "What a longing I have to see the places I remember so well—London, Bath, Edinburgh, and Elgin," Alexander wrote to his mother. Once in the United Kingdom, he delighted in showing his bride his old homes and haunts in England and Scotland. But the honeymoon trip to Britain soon turned into a working vacation. Bell was becoming famous as an inventor, and everyone in Britain wanted to see a demonstration of his amazing telephone—even the queen herself.

On January 14, 1878, Queen Victoria slowly entered the Council Room at Osborne House, along with two of her children—Prince Arthur and Princess Beatrice. The 58-year-old monarch wore a black silk gown and widow's cap. After receiving Her Majesty's invitation, Bell had traveled to the royal residence on the Isle of Wight to set up a telephone demonstration. The queen sat and listened to telephone conversations coming in from nearby buildings and even the neighboring town. At one point during the demonstration, Bell touched the queen's hand to offer her the telephone so she could listen in on a song. Onlookers were shocked by his violation of royal rules. No one was permitted to touch the queen! The error in etiquette didn't seem to dull Victoria's excitement over the telephone. She wrote in her diary that night that it was "most extraordinary."

ABOVE: **Mabel Bell holds her three-month-old daughter, Elsie May.** Library of Congress, LC-G9-Z1-155,853-A

RIGHT: **Alexander Graham Bell shortly after his marriage to Mabel Hubbard in 1877.** Library of Congress, LC-G9-Z1-144,963-A

In Bell's day, nearly every city and town had a Western Union telegraph office.
Library of Congress, LC-DIG-hec-02415

A lot happened during the year Mabel and Alexander spent abroad. News of the telephone spread throughout Europe. But showing off the invention wasn't the only reason the Bells had stayed in Europe so long. Their daughter Elsie May was born on May 8, 1878, in London.

By the time the young family arrived back in America, there were Bell telephones in hundreds of businesses and even a few private residences. American author Mark Twain had a telephone at home. Even the US president who'd once wondered why anyone would want a telephone now called it "one of the greatest events since creation." The first White House telephone was installed in 1879, and President Hayes's first call was to Alexander Graham Bell.

Court Battles

The telephone made Bell famous and wealthy. But many imposter inventors and dishonest businessmen tried to cash in on the success of the "speaking telegraph." Bell complained about it in a letter to Mabel in 1878: "The more fame a man gets for an invention, the more does he become a target for the world to shoot at."

The first to take a shot at the Bell Telephone Company was Western Union. The telegraph giant had missed its chance to buy Bell's telephone patent and now feared for its future. The telephone was going to replace the telegraph. Western Union Telegraph Company wanted the Bell Telephone Company out of their way, so they teamed up with inventors Elisha Gray and Thomas Edison. The two men came up with a competing telephone design that Western Union quickly began installing across the country. Western Union also accused Bell of not being the telephone's inventor. Newspapers printed stories calling Gray the true inventor. Edison and Gray claimed that Bell couldn't have invented the telephone because he wasn't an electrician.

Western Union's bullying worked. The Bell Telephone Company was nearing failure. To fight back, Bell Telephone sued Western Union for illegal use of its telephone patent. Bell and Watson testified in court, convincingly detailing how they'd invented the telephone. Smelling defeat, Western Union gave up. But it was only the first of many hundreds of court battles that the Bell Telephone Company would have to fight over two long decades. The total amount of courtroom paperwork was more than 9 feet (3 m) high! But Bell and his telephone patent won every legal case.

"The inventor is a man who looks around upon the world and is not contented with things as they are," Bell explained in a speech. "He wants to improve whatever he sees, he wants to benefit the world." Inventing technology and educating people who were deaf were the two things that he wanted to keep doing—not running Bell Telephone Company. Besides testifying in court, Bell didn't have much to do with the company that carried his name. And as he told his father-in-law, "business (which is hateful to me at all times) would fetter me as an inventor."

Bell was upset by all the lies questioning his invention. The untruths made him want to prove his worth as an inventor to the world. "I can't bear to hear that even friends should think that I stumbled upon an invention and that there is no more good in me," he wrote Mabel while traveling. He didn't have reason to worry. He would go on to invent devices that record sound and aid the sick, and vehicles that travel through the air and water. But he would never fully escape the shadow of his own fame as the inventor of the telephone.

The Sound of Sunshine

Bell said, "Discoveries and inventions arise from the observation of little things." One

········ Ma Bell ········

The Bell Telephone Company formed by Bell, Watson, Hubbard, and Sanders in 1877 nearly failed. When Western Union Telegraph Company entered the telephone business in 1877 using transmitters developed by Thomas Edison and receivers designed by Elisha Gray, the giant company quickly gobbled up much of the market. The Bell Telephone Company battled back by using improved transmitters and suing Western Union for illegally infringing on Bell's patents. In 1879, Western Union recognized Bell's patents and sold its telephone business to the Bell Telephone Company.

In 1885, the American Telephone and Telegraph Company (AT&T) was created to operate the long-distance network of the Bell Telephone Company. AT&T eventually became the parent company of the Bell System, including AT&T and other telephone companies that supplied phone service to nearly every home and business in the United States. If you wanted telephone service, you had to get it from "Ma Bell."

In 1974, the US government sued AT&T, charging that it was an illegal monopoly. AT&T was broken up in 1984 into smaller regional "Baby Bell" companies, such as Southwestern Bell Corporation (SBC), and AT&T became a provider of long-distance service. Today AT&T Inc. is still one of the largest telecommunications companies in the world. It provides data, video, and voice communications services to businesses, governments, and homes across the globe.

Bad weather caused problems for the mess of telephone and telegraph wires strung throughout cities. New York Historical Society

such observation he made was that America's streets were becoming a mess of crisscrossing telephone wires. He wondered if all those wires were really necessary. What if there was a way to transmit speech without wires, using beams of light instead? The answer to this question was an invention that Alexander Graham Bell considered to be the most important of his life, even greater than the telephone: the wireless **photophone**.

By late 1879, Alexander and Mabel were living in Washington, DC. It was there that Bell started working on the photophone with a young man named Charles Sumner Tainter. Tainter had worked at the same shop that Thomas Watson had, but he made optical equipment. Together, Bell and Tainter built a light-powered phone using mirrors, lenses, and an element that conducted electricity called selenium. Taken together, all these

Bell's Photophone

Just like the telephone, Bell's photophone sent sound across distances. But instead of sending it along wires, the photophone used light. On a standard plug-in landline telephone, a magnet on a flexible membrane within a copper-wire circuit creates a speech-sending undulating electric current. Bell's photophone instead used light-sensitive selenium and a beam of sunlight to connect a transmitter to a receiver. Selenium is a photoelectric element. Its resistance, or ability to conduct electricity, is changed when light shines on it.

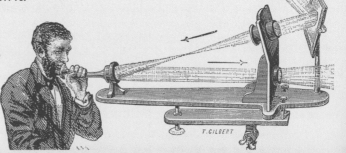

Bell's photophone transmitter used a reflective vibrating membrane at the end of the mouthpiece to create and send an undulating stream of light. Wikimedia Commons

pieces completed a circuit from speaker to listener, like a telephone, but there were no wires involved.

After months of tinkering, Bell and Tainter had a working invention that could send voice messages hundreds of yards. Proud of his new invention, Bell poetically wrote his father: "I have heard articulate speech produced by sunlight! I have heard a ray of the sun laugh and cough and sing!" Alexander was so proud of his invention that he wanted to name his and Mabel's second child Photophone! Luckily for their daughter, Mabel talked him out of it. The Bells' second daughter was born February 15, 1880, and named Marian—but they called her Daisy.

Bell imagined that the light-powered photophone would quickly replace the wire-bound telephone, allowing even ships at sea to communicate. But the photophone never became a practical device in his lifetime. When he invented it, people still lit their homes with gas lamps and rode in horse-drawn carriages. They simply weren't ready for something as futuristic as the photophone.

Still, it wasn't a complete loss. The photophone demonstrated principles that were later developed into fiber optics and wireless mobile phones. It would take nearly a century, however, for technology—and the public—to catch up to the imagination of Alexander Graham Bell.

TRAGEDY AND INSPIRATION

IMAGINATION AND observation weren't the only sources of Bell's inspiration. Unfortunately, so was tragedy. And it was the American tragedy of a president who lay dying from a bullet wound that inspired Bell to invent the telephonic probe. The year was 1881, and President James Garfield—who had been in office only a few months—was shot by a mentally ill man named Charles Guiteau at a Washington, DC, train station.

Garfield survived the shooting, but one of the bullets went deep into his body. In 1881, there were no X-rays and little belief in the new theory that germs cause infection. Doctors crudely tried to find the bullet by poking unwashed fingers and unsterilized

This 1881 newspaper illustration shows Bell (standing second from right) listening through an earpiece receiver for sounds of a bullet as a doctor moves the handheld metal detector over the abdomen of the dying President Garfield.
Library of Congress, LC-USZ62-134586

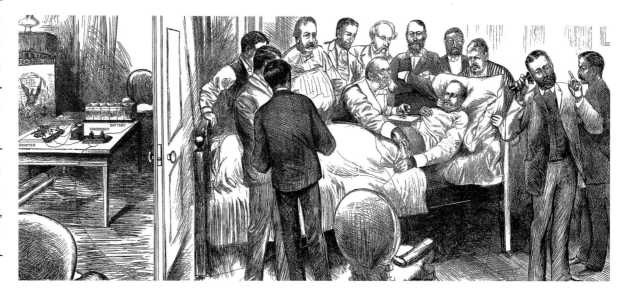

instruments into Garfield's wound. The president's body quickly raged with infection, and the bullet remained lodged. "The whole world watched," Bell remembered. "And hopes and fears filled every passing hour. No one could venture to predict the end so long as the position of the bullet remained unknown."

Bell went to Garfield's bedside to try to find the bullet with his latest invention, the metal detector. It was simply a telephone earpiece, or receiver, hooked up to an electromagnet. When the device passed something metallic —in this case, a bullet—the tone coming through the receiver would change. The inventor had successfully tested it by searching for bullets that had been shot into slabs of meat. But Bell's device was unable to locate the bullet inside President Garfield. Eighty miserable days after being shot, Garfield died. If he had been left to recover on his own and had not been poked and prodded, it's possible he might have pulled through.

Why did the metal detector miss Garfield's bullet? It's hard to know for sure, but it's likely that Garfield lay on a bed with coiled springs. The metal bedsprings would have interfered with the readings. Bell's device was later successfully used to find bullets in other patients, including World War I soldiers.

The events in Washington inspired Bell to invent a similar bullet detector called the telephonic probe. It saved the lives of many gunshot victims and soldiers before X-ray machines. "Certainly no man can have a higher incentive than the hope of relieving suffering and saving life," he humbly remarked. Unfortunately, his own family's suffering would soon become his next incentive to invent.

GRIEF AND INVENTION

WHILE PRESIDENT Garfield lay dying, Mabel was giving birth to a third child. The Bells were spending the summer in Massachusetts while Alexander was in Washington working on his bullet detector. Mabel had a baby boy on August 15, 1881. But baby Edward, named for Alexander's brother, was born too soon.

ABOVE: **Thousands of people with the disease polio, including this boy in 1955, were treated in iron lungs.** Otis Historical Archives, National Museum of Health and Medicine, NCP4145

RIGHT: **This drawing by Bell shows his idea for the vacuum jacket.** Library of Congress, MSS51268

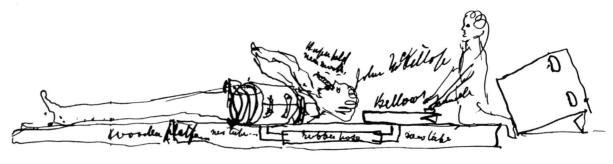

The premature baby died from breathing difficulties within a few hours.

Bell channeled his grief into work, inventing a device to aid people having trouble breathing. He called the world's first artificial **respirator** a vacuum jacket. His invented breathing apparatus was a hinged iron tube that snugly closed around a patient's chest. A hand pump changed the air pressure inside the metal cylinder, squeezing and releasing the patient's chest, mechanically forcing air in and out of the lungs. In later years, the vacuum jacket would evolve into the iron lung, a breathing machine used for people with polio.

Unfortunately, no new invention could save Mabel and Alexander's fourth child. Robert Bell was also born prematurely on November 17, 1883. "Poor little one," Mabel wrote. "It was so pretty and struggled so hard to live, opened his eyes once or twice to the world and then passed away." Alexander and Mabel would have no more children.

The year 1883 didn't pass without some happy events for Alexander Graham Bell. He had long dreamed of opening a new kind of school for children who were deaf, one where kids would learn to speak using the Visible Speech system, and he'd spent years planning and training a teacher. In the fall of 1883, Bell finally opened the school in a brick building surrounded by gardens in Washington, DC.

WORK THE PROBLEM

"Necessity is the mother of invention." You've probably heard that old saying. The saying means that problems and challenges inspire people to problem solve and find better ways to do something. Car accidents led engineers to install seatbelts, diseases drove doctors to find medicines, and so on. This was true for Alexander Graham Bell, too. Many of his inventions were inspired by challenges and tragedies in his life and the lives of those he cared about. From finding ways to communicate with his deaf mother to inventing a breathing machine, when Bell recognized a problem he tried to solve it. And you can, too!

You'll Need

- Paper
- Pen or pencil
- Brain power

1. Over the next few days, pay attention to what frustrates you. Notice when you think:

   Someone should figure out a better way to _____ .

   Why can't they make a better _____ ?

2. Keep a list of the objects and situations from step 1.

3. Choose one of your listed problems to solve, inventions to create, or processes to improve. It can be something simple, like changing the dog bowl so it no longer splashes onto the floor or working out a way to save ten minutes in the morning so you can sleep longer. You can also choose a big challenge you'll want to patent, like improving a Frisbee or designing a self-sharpening pencil.

4. Keep a journal, like Alexander Graham Bell did, with your ideas. You can sketch out designs and document failures and successes. Good luck!

Alexander Graham Bell (back row, center) with students and faculty of his school for deaf children.
Library of Congress, LC-USZ62-115828

Understanding for Everyone

6

Sounds of schoolyard recess filled the air around the old-fashioned building in Washington, DC. Young boys and girls played in the small school's garden and lawn. About half a dozen or so of the children in the schoolyard were deaf. But the children who couldn't hear played with the kids who could, reading lips and speaking as best they could. When recess was over, the students who could hear—all kindergarteners—shuffled into the downstairs classroom. Elsie and Daisy Bell were two of the kindergarteners who attended their father's school. The six students who were deaf climbed the stairs to the second-floor room in Mr. Bell's school.

The upstairs room wasn't like most 1883 classrooms. The students shared a low table instead of sitting separately in bolted-down desks. Pictures, games, toys, and a soft carpet filled the classroom. There were cozy, interesting, and brightly colored things to stimulate the students' senses of sight and touch. Many objects around the room were labeled in both English and Visible Speech. The teacher, a young woman, helped the students learn to lip-read by reading the names on the labels. And the Visible Speech symbols helped the students learn to speak.

The Bell daughters, Daisy and Elsie, with their governess in 1885. Library of Congress, LC-USZ62-122254

Opening the school had been a dream of Bell's for many years. He had never lost interest in deaf education, what he called "my life-work." Even while honeymooning and demonstrating the telephone to Queen Victoria in 1878, he had found time to open another school for the deaf in Greenock, Scotland. He wrote Mabel from Scotland, "I have been so happy in my little school, happier than at any time since the telephone took my mind away from this work."

But telephone work would again take Bell's mind away from educating people who were deaf. The constant court battles over the telephone's patents kept him from being able to run the school. Sadly, Mr. Bell's school closed after two short—though successful—years. He wrote that the school's failure was the most disappointing experience of his life.

THE DEAF EDUCATION DEBATE

BELL WASN'T a man to let disappointment hold him back for long. And he would continue to do everything he could to help break down the barriers between people who were deaf and those who could hear. He knew firsthand how most deaf people were cut off from society. His mother was deaf, his wife was deaf, and he had personal relationships with many of his deaf students and their families.

"Who can picture the isolation of their lives?" Bell passionately asked in a speech. "[Imagine] the solitude of an intellectual being in the midst of a crowd of happy beings with whom he can not communicate and who cannot communicate with him.... The sense of loneliness in the midst of so many is oppressive."

During Bell's time, many children who were deaf didn't go to school at all. Few places had public schools for the deaf, and private schools were too expensive for most parents. Deaf children were often considered "slow" or learning disabled. Many communicated using their own systems of gestures and grunts that people outside their family couldn't understand. Those students lucky enough to get an education were usually sent away to boarding schools. But Bell believed that regular day schools were better for deaf children, since he thought that children living at home with their families would be more motivated to learn to speak and lip-read.

Bell believed that children who were deaf should be taught to speak and read lips so they could live more independent lives—just as his wife, Mabel, had done. But his strong beliefs were challenged by another pioneer of deaf education, Edward Gallaudet. Gallaudet was the youngest son of Thomas Hopkins Gallaudet, the founder of America's first school for the deaf. Like Alexander Graham Bell, Edward Gallaudet's mother was deaf. But

The Audiometer

An **audiometer** is a device for measuring a person's hearing. The audiometer combined Bell's two great passions: inventing and helping people who were hearing-impaired. He invented the audiometer in 1879 and presented it to the National Academy of Sciences in 1885. It worked by creating an electric current in a wire coil connected in a circuit to a telephone receiver. Patients held the receiver up to their ears and listened as the loudness of the sound was varied. The unit used to measure the relative loudness of sounds, the bel or decibel, is named for Alexander Graham Bell.

unlike Bell, Gallaudet believed that people who were deaf should not be taught to speak. He thought sign language was the most practical and rewarding form of communication for the deaf community. The argument was about the best way to educate deaf children: teaching them sign language or to read lips and speak. Bell and Gallaudet became rivals in this debate over deaf education called "oralism versus manualism." The topic is still controversial among educators and parents today. For those who champion sign language and its importance in deaf culture, Bell was someone on the wrong side of history.

To help promote his ideas about educating the deaf, Bell founded the American Association to Promote the Teaching of Speech to the Deaf. When the association was started in 1890, only about 40 percent of deaf students learned to speak as part of their education. Thirty years later, that percentage had doubled. The organization was eventually renamed the Alexander Graham Bell Association for the Deaf and Hard of Hearing, in honor of its founder. Today it remains an organization dedicated to "advocating independence through listening and talking."

Bell worked to promote deaf education in the United States and abroad for his entire life. He donated nearly half a million dollars ($14 million in today's money) to charities and schools for the deaf. He also invented the audiometer, a device to measure how well a person can hear, and used it to test the hearing of hundreds of people. Many were children who'd

American Sign Language

American Sign Language (ASL) is how most deaf people communicate in North America today. It allows people to communicate through seeing, not hearing. ASL uses hand signs as well as facial expressions and body postures.

Sign language is different from finger spelling words or creating sentences by stringing together signs that mean specific words. The sign language used in a place is often completely unrelated to the language spoken there. American Sign Language uses different signs in different ways and combinations than British Sign Language—even though English is spoken in both places. ASL is its own complete language with rules of grammar and vocabulary. It works dif-

ferently than spoken or written languages. For example, there is no sign for a question mark in ASL. English speakers know it's a question when someone raises the pitch of his or her voice. "The dog is lost" sounds different than "The dog is lost?" when spoken aloud. ASL users ask a question by raising their eyebrows, widening their eyes, and leaning forward. Communicating with sign language is important to most people who are deaf. According to the National Association of the Deaf, "ASL is the backbone of the American deaf culture."

These kids are learning to sign "I love you" in American Sign Language.
Tom Uhlman Media

been labeled lazy but were actually struggling in school because they couldn't hear well.

"Bell was never happier than when he was holding a deaf child in his arms," a family friend commented. And Bell was never too busy to help find a way to educate a deaf child. He'd created a glove with letters of the alphabet written on the fingers to teach Georgie, the five-year-old son of Thomas Sanders, to finger spell words back in Boston. And Bell would arrange for a miracle-working instructor to tutor a young girl who was deaf and blind named Helen Keller.

A DOOR THROUGH DARKNESS

CAPTAIN ARTHUR H. Keller was no stranger to war—or defeat. He'd been an officer in the Confederate army in the American Civil War. Now he and his wife, Kate, were losing a battle with their own child. Little Helen was both blind and deaf.

Like many other deaf children, Helen didn't know how to speak. By age six, she had grown into a wild, angry child—kicking, scratching, and choking out screams to try to get what she wanted. What would become of Helen? Many like her were abandoned to horrific institutions that housed severely mentally ill people. But Captain and Kate Keller were told that a famous man and educator of the deaf might

MEANINGFUL GESTURES

Have you ever seen someone using sign language? Many events have sign language interpreters who sign while someone is speaking. More and more parents are teaching their babies to sign, too. Here are a few basic American Sign Language signs. Learn them and make a new friend!

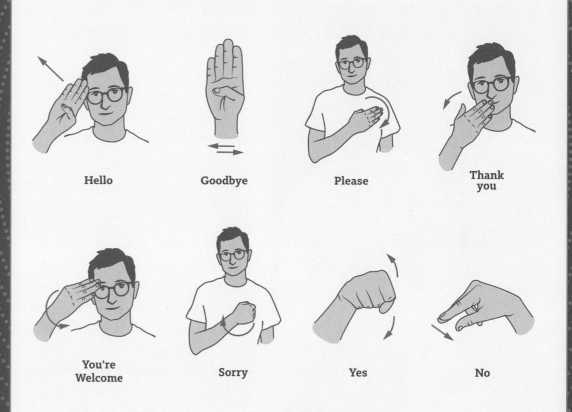

Hello Goodbye Please Thank you

You're Welcome Sorry Yes No

DO MORE: YouTube is a great resource for learning American Sign Language. Many signs involve movement, so video is perfect for that. Check it out!

Eight-year-old Helen Keller and her tutor Anne Sullivan in 1888.
Courtesy New England Historic Genealogical Society

be able to help their daughter. The Kellers decided to take Helen to meet Alexander Graham Bell.

Helen liked taking trips. She couldn't see the scenery or hear the city sounds, but the jostling feeling of trains and bumpy horse carriages was exciting. It was a long trip from her home in Tuscumbia, Alabama, to Washington, DC. Once at Bell's home, Helen climbed up and sat on the knee of this large man her parents had brought her to meet. Bell placed his watch in her hand and made it chime, which he knew she would be able to feel. He immediately understood the crude signs and gestures she used to try to communicate. He saw intelligence and a bright spirit in this little girl completely alone inside herself. Helen felt Bell's kindness, empathy, and understanding of her world. The two became friends at once. She would later write of meeting him, "That interview would be the door through which I should pass from darkness into light."

Bell told the Kellers that he thought Helen could be taught to communicate—given the right teacher. He recommended contacting Perkins School for the Blind in Boston to help find a tutor. Twenty-year-old Anne Sullivan was sent to the Keller home to teach Helen. Within a month, Helen understood that the words Anne was finger spelling into her hand were names for the things around her. This

········ Helen Keller ········

Helen Keller could see and hear when she was born, but she became very sick as a baby. Her illness destroyed both her sight and her hearing at about age 1½. She grew into a child full of frustration and confusion about the world around her. Thanks to her teacher Anne Sullivan, Helen Keller eventually learned to communicate with the outside world.

Keller helped to found the Massachusetts Commission for the Blind and raised more money for the American Foundation for the Blind than any other person. She went to college and became an author. She wrote a number of books, including *The Story of My Life* (1902), that have been translated into dozens of languages. *The Miracle Worker* is a play and movie that dramatizes her childhood.

breakthrough allowed Helen to finally communicate with the world.

Soon Helen and Anne could "talk" by finger spelling. Then Helen learned to read and write by feeling raised letters with the Braille alphabet. "Dear Mr. Bell," she wrote at age eight. "I am glad to write you a letter.... I can read stories in my book. I can write and spell and count." Helen knew that most people spoke with their mouths, not with sign language or by finger spelling. She learned to read lips by placing her fingers on the lips and throat of the speaker. She could sense the vibrations when words were spoken and could feel the shape of the mouth. Amazingly, she was able to use this skill to learn to speak around age 10.

A Lifelong Friendship

Bell closely followed Helen's progress. She was living proof that people who were deaf and blind could learn to communicate with the right kind of teaching. Bell was grateful for the public attention that Helen's life brought to deaf education. And while many called Anne Sullivan a "miracle worker," Bell knew better. It was Sullivan's creative and inventive ways of teaching that had broken through Helen's isolation. Bell believed others could benefit from such methods, too.

Helen's famous breakthrough had come when she finally connected the cool water

flowing out of the pump with the letters "W-A-T-E-R" that her teacher spelled into her hand. Anne Sullivan "spoke" to Helen as they explored the garden and house, just as you would with a child who can hear and is learning to talk. Sullivan didn't always stop to explain new words. She let Helen figure out what they meant through **context**, as a hearing child does.

Helen Keller and Alexander Graham Bell were lifelong friends. Wikimedia Commons

Helen Keller and Alexander Graham Bell became lifelong friends. In 1893, he traveled with Helen and Anne Sullivan to Niagara Falls, on the border between the United States and Canada. Standing near the falls, Bell gave Helen a feather pillow. She held the pillow against her chest, and it magnified the vibrations she felt from the powerful falling water. "You can never imagine how I felt when I stood in the presence of Niagara until you have the same mysterious sensations yourself," Helen wrote her mother. "I could hardly realize that it was water that I felt rushing and plunging with impetuous fury at my feet. It seemed as if it were some living thing rushing on to some terrible fate.... I had the same feeling once before when I first stood by the great ocean and felt its waves beating against the shore. I suppose you feel so, too, when you gaze up to the stars in the stillness of the night, do you not?" These were amazing observations for a not quite 13-year-old girl who couldn't see or hear what she was describing.

When Keller and Bell were together, they were constantly finger spelling back and forth. He taught her about science and his work. "He makes you feel that if you only had a little more time, you, too, might be an inventor," she wrote. He helped pay for her to attend college, and she visited the Bells' home many times throughout her life. When she wrote her autobiography, she dedicated it "to Alexander Graham Bell. Who has taught the deaf to speak and enabled the listening ear to hear speech from the Atlantic to the Rockies, I dedicate this Story of My Life."

Helen Keller understood that educating people who were deaf was Bell's lifework. Bell once said, "One would think I had never done anything worthwhile but the telephone. That is because it is a money-making invention. It is a pity so many people make money the **criterion** of success. I wish my experiences had resulted in enabling the deaf to speak with less difficulty. That would have made me truly

.... The Volta Prize ....

The first battery to make electric power from chemicals was called a voltaic pile. It was invented in 1800 by an Italian chemist named Alessandro Volta. The unit of measure for electricity, the volt, is named in Volta's honor, as is the Volta Prize, which Alexander Graham Bell won in 1880. French emperor Napoleon Bonaparte established the prize to honor Volta and recognize achievements in electricity.

An Alessandro Volta battery.
Courtesy "GuidoB" via Wikimedia Commons

FOUR-CENT BATTERY

Batteries power all sorts of things these days, from flashlights to hybrid cars. The first battery to make electric power from chemicals was called a voltaic pile. It's a stack of metal discs sandwiched with acid-soaked cloth. The acid conducts electricity between the metal discs and through an electric circuit. You can make a working voltaic battery using copper pennies, zinc washers, and vinegar as an acid.

You'll Need

- 4 pennies (1982 or older if American; 1996 or older if Canadian)
- Coffee filter or paper towels
- Pen or pencil
- Scissors
- White vinegar
- Shallow dish
- 4 zinc-covered (galvanized) washers
- LED lightbulb with two lead wires
- Electrical or duct tape

1. Copper pennies will be the battery's positive terminal. Make sure your US pennies are 1982 or older (1996 or older for Canadian pennies). Newer pennies don't have enough copper in them.

2. Trace a penny on the coffee filter paper or paper towel. Do this three more times and then cut out the discs.

3. Pour some of the vinegar into a shallow dish. It's the acidic electrolyte.

4. Build your battery cells. Start with a penny. Then dip a paper disc into the vinegar. It needs to be soaked through, but not dripping. (Blotting it on a napkin or paper towel can help.) Place the wet paper disc on top of the penny. Set a zinc washer on top of the wet paper. This is one cell.

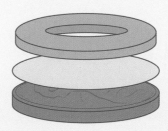

5. Repeat step 4, making four penny-paper-washer sandwiches.

6. Stack the four sandwiches, penny on top of washer.

7. Hold the wire ends of an LED lightbulb to each end of your battery to complete a circuit. The lightbulb is polarized, so its positive end needs to touch the top zinc washer and its negative end the bottom copper penny. If it isn't lighting up, swap the wires and try again. Another problem could be a short caused by electrolyte (the vinegar) spilling over from one cell to another. Wipe the sides dry, or rebuild with less-damp paper discs, and try again.

8. Once the bulb lights up, tape everything together. How long does your battery keep the LED lit?

happy." At age 70, he wrote that "recognition of my work for and interest in the education of the deaf has always been more pleasing to me than even recognition of my work with the telephone."

TEAMWORK AND COMPETITION

In 1880, Bell was awarded the $10,000 Volta Prize by the French government for his invention of the telephone. He used the prize money to fund a laboratory near his home in Washington, DC, and named it the Volta Laboratory after the award. He hired Sumner Tainter and his chemist cousin, Chichester Bell, to work at the lab. Bell's work with Thomas Watson had taught him the value of scientific teamwork, and he backed that belief with money. "In scientific researches, there are no unsuccessful experiments; every experiment contains a lesson," he wrote. "If we don't get the results anticipated and stop right there, it is the man that is unsuccessful, not the experiment."

One early autumn day in 1881, Sumner Tainter, Chichester Bell, and Alexander Graham Bell were gathered in the new Volta

BELOW: Thomas Alva Edison listening to what was said to be his favorite invention, the phonograph, in 1888. Notice the light-colored wax recording cylinders. Wikimedia Commons

BELOW RIGHT: Photographing sound in 1884 at the Volta Laboratory. Wikimedia Commons

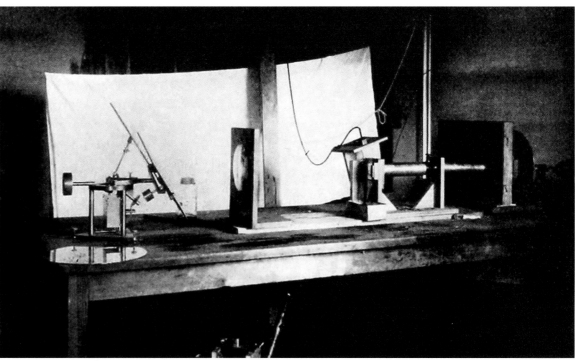

Laboratory. The trio had been working on improving an invention that could record sounds and play them back—a **phonograph**. They'd been tinkering with their machine for months now. The men hoped that the contraption could finally play back a clear-sounding recording. Now it was time to test it. The device was switched on, and out came a perfectly understandable sentence: "I am a **graphophone**, and my mother was a phonograph." It worked! The Volta Lab team members congratulated one another.

········ The Phonograph ········

Thomas Edison invented the phonograph in 1877. His invention used a tinfoil-covered cylinder shaped like a can to record and play back sound. Attached to the cylinder was a needle connected to a vibrating diaphragm. A hand crank spun the cylinder. When a person spoke into a mouthpiece, the sound waves made the diaphragm and needle vibrate and carve dents into the spinning cylinder's tinfoil. Listeners played back recorded sounds using a different needle, also attached to a diaphragm set against the cylinder. The needle rode up and down over the dents on the spinning cylinder, making the needle and diaphragm vibrate and reproducing the recorded sounds. But Edison's original phonograph didn't sound very good, and the tinfoil indentations were ruined after a few playings.

The trio at Volta Laboratory improved on Edison's invention in many ways. They called their better version a graphophone. The Volta team quickly found that a wax-covered cylinder lasted longer than a tinfoil one. The needle cut a permanent groove into the wax instead of just making flimsy dents in tinfoil. And they eventually patented the first flat, round, hard wax discs—records!—for recording sounds. The Volta team also invented a flexible zigzagging needle instead of a stiff one that rode up and down. This greatly improved the quality of the phonograph's sound.

Record players like the graphophone invented by Alexander Graham Bell and the Volta Lab were a kind of home entertainment system.
Wikimedia Commons

PIZZA BOX PHONOGRAPH

Record player technology hasn't changed all that much since Alexander Graham Bell's day. Records themselves are no longer made of wax. They're pressed out of vinyl, a kind of plastic, and have less background noise. But the basics are the same. Tiny bumps and dips in the grooves of the flat disc re-create the recorded sound when a needle rides up and down over them and creates vibrations amplified by a speaker. The early phonographs didn't have speakers. A horn attached to the diaphragm-holding sound box amplified the music. To play a record, the listener turned a crank on the device to wind it up like a clock. You too can listen to a record without electricity in this activity.

You'll Need

- Record from a thrift store or one that can be scratched
- Pencil with a sharpened end
- Pizza box or other sturdy, flat cardboard box
- Ruler
- Scissors
- Strong tape (optional)
- Pushpin
- Plastic drinking cup
- Friend

1. Choose a pencil that fits snugly into the record's center (spindle) hole. Put the pencil's sharpened end through the hole of the record. Turn a pizza box upside down, and then push the pencil though the bottom of the pizza box to make a hole.

2. Cut a 2-inch (5-cm) square or circle out of a cardboard scrap (or the pizza box lid). Use scissors to poke a hole in its center. Lift the pencil and record out of the hole in the pizza box and push the cardboard circle or square onto the pencil, as shown.

3. Return the pencil into the hole of the pizza box and push it all the way through so the pencil tip reaches the other side of the box. Give it a spin using the pencil spindle. If the pencil slips inside the hole, use some tape to secure the pencil to the record. Your turntable is ready!

4. Poke the pushpin through the bottom corner of a plastic drinking cup, as shown. If it's loose, tape it in place. This is your needle, vibrating sound box, and amplifying horn!

5. Have a friend spin the record spindle as smoothly as possible to spin the record clockwise. It might take a bit of practice. While the record is spinning, hold the cup so that the pushpin goes into a groove of the record at an angle. It takes a light touch! How does it sound? How could you improve it?

Thomas Edison had invented the phonograph four years earlier. But Edison's phonograph didn't work very well. One scientist called the device marvelous but useless. Edison soon gave up on it, believing it would never make money.

Bell disagreed. He decided to turn Edison's crude invention into a practical machine that recorded sounds and played them back. (Bell called his invention a graphophone instead of a phonograph.) A better-working phonograph would not only allow people to record and listen to music and speeches but also give Bell a chance to beat Edison at his own game. Edison had invented a carbon telephone transmitter for Western Union that had improved on Bell's telephone design. Now Bell had improved an invention of Edison's! An irritated Edison ended up having to buy the rights to Bell's graphophone patent so he could improve the phonograph and turn his own invention into a profitable product.

"THE WORLD AND ALL THAT IS IN IT"

BELL WAS happy to fund scientific research. But he also understood the importance of communication in science. The inventor decided to help scientists keep up with new discoveries and findings by rescuing a failing magazine called *Science*. Thomas Edison had funded the magazine's start-up in 1880, but he stopped supporting it when it failed to make money. So Bell and his father-in-law, Gardiner Greene Hubbard, took over the magazine and kept it going. The magazine has been published ever since, and today *Science* is one of the most important scientific journals in the world. Bell and Hubbard also went on to start another magazine that's still around today: the *National Geographic Magazine*.

BELOW: The Volta Lab invented many things, including this graphophone. A recording was created on a spinning wax cylinder by speaking into the mouthpiece while pushing on a foot pedal. To listen to the recording, the mouthpiece was replaced by the earphones. Wikimedia Commons

RIGHT: *Science* has been one of the world's most important journals for more than 125 years. *Science*, August 27, 1881

Bell wanted everyone—not just scientists—to better understand the world. To help in that goal, he and his father-in-law helped set up the National Geographic Society in 1888. Bell took part in shaping *National Geographic* into a magazine packed full of dazzling photographs, illustrations, and maps. "The world and all that is in it is our theme," he announced. He eventually became president of the society in 1899.

The young man who took on the day-to-day job of running the magazine was Gilbert Grosvenor. Bell advised the young editor to show the world as it was. This meant including photographs that offended some readers, such as images of indigenous people wearing less clothing than 19th-century Americans considered decent. Grosvenor successfully guided *National Geographic* for more than half a century. He also became part of the Bell family; Gilbert and Bell's daughter Elsie were married in 1900. In 1905, younger daughter Daisy Bell also married a man she met through the National Geographic Society, a botanist named David Fairchild. Alexander and Mabel would eventually have ten grandchildren.

With *National Geographic* in good hands and a new century underway, Bell felt it was time to move on. He stepped down as president of the society and spent his time on his other interests, as well as with his family. He found a place where he could do all these things, far from the pressures and summer heat of Washington, DC. Beinn Bhreagh was calling.

Alexander, Mabel, and their daughters Elsie (left) and Daisy in 1885.
Library of Congress, LC-G9-Z4-116,794-T

Alexander Graham Bell with his family and friends in Baddeck, Nova Scotia, around 1890. Bell is in the front row, second from right, and holding a hat. Library of Congress, LC-USZ62-117580

Into the Air, Water, and History

7

Arthur McCurdy was frustrated with telephones, or at least with the one in his newspaper office. The editor of the *Cape Breton Island Reporter* couldn't get the blasted thing on the wall to work. McCurdy was trying to talk by telephone to his brother, Lucien. But Lucien couldn't hear McCurdy's voice. The darn telephone had been working fine this morning! Now what was McCurdy supposed to do? There wasn't any telephone repair service in Baddeck, where he lived. The village was on Cape Breton Island in the Canadian province of **Nova Scotia**. It was a remote place in 1885.

A man passing by the office window noticed the newspaperman battling with his phone. Next thing McCurdy knew, a tall gentleman with dark bushy hair and whiskers was in his office asking what was the matter. McCurdy told the stranger the problem, explaining that his brother didn't seem to be hearing what was said into the telephone. The beefy gentleman walked over to the telephone and picked up the mouthpiece. He unscrewed it, fiddled with the transmitter, and put it back together.

Miraculously, the telephone then worked fine and the McCurdy brothers could speak to each other. When a grateful Arthur McCurdy asked the stranger how he knew how to fix a telephone, the man smiled. "My name is Alexander Graham Bell," he said.

Alexander and Mabel were in Canada on vacation. Alexander loved Nova Scotia. The land, climate, and people reminded him of his Scottish homeland. He wasn't the first to notice the similarity. Nova Scotia means "New Scotland" in **Gaelic**, the ancient language of Scotland. The Bells and their extended family often visited Baddeck. During one visit, Alexander and his cousin Charles Bell were hiking near a low mountain that reached out into Baddeck Bay. The peninsula of land surrounded by water had fascinated Bell from afar. Now that he was seeing it up close, it captivated him. When the cousins found a sparkling small waterfall during the hike, it seemed to seal the deal. Alexander and Mabel purchased the land overlooking the sea and named it Beinn Bhreagh (pronounced BEN vreeah), which means "beautiful mountain" in Scottish Gaelic.

"Beautiful dense woods of fir, spruce, birch, and maple cover the place from five hundred feet down to a height of about twenty feet from the water's edge," wrote Mabel to her mother. "The children are delighted with their free, wild life here." They could swim and hike—and have pets. One little lamb followed the children everywhere and was always trying to get in the house.

Alexander had become a US citizen in 1882, but he loved Nova Scotia and spent

Beinn Bhreagh, the Bell estate in Nova Scotia. Library of Congress, LOT 11533-30 no. 2

TOP LEFT: **Mabel and Alexander rowing in the small harbor near their estate.** Wikimedia Commons

ABOVE: **Beinn Bhreagh, the Bells' Nova Scotia estate.** Courtesy Donald Hamm

SPEAK LIKE A SCOT

Gaelic is an ancient language, with deep roots in Ireland. When Irish colonists moved to Scotland around the year 500 CE, they brought Gaelic with them. Over the centuries Irish and Scottish Gaelic grew different from each other. And when England began invading Scotland and Ireland in the 1100s, the English language of the conquerors took hold. Today, Irish Gaelic is the official language of Ireland and is often just called Irish.

Scottish Gaelic is still around, too, especially in the names of places like Alexander Graham Bell's home, Beinn Bhreagh. Why not learn a few other Scottish Gaelic phrases?

English	Scottish Gaelic	How to Say It
Hello	Halò	*ha-LOW*
How are you?	Ciamar a tha sibh?	*KEM-mer uh HAH shiv?*
I'm well, thanks.	Tha gu math, tapadh leibh.	*HAH guh MAH, TAH-puh LEH-eev*
My name is…	S mise…	*SMIH-shuh…*
What's your name?	Dè an t-ainm a tha oirbh?	*Jeh un TAH-num uh HAW-ruv?*
Good morning	Madainn mhath	*MAT-een vah*
Good afternoon/ evening	Feasgar math	*FES-ker mah*
Good night	Oidhche mhath	*EYE-chuh vah*
Please	Ma 'se ur toil e	*mah sheh oor TUL-leh*
Thank you	Tapadh leat	*TAH-puh LAHT*
Excuse me	Gabhaibh mo leisgeul	*GAHV-iv moe LESH-kul*

much of his later life there. "Though I cannot claim to be a Canadian," he once said, "I have a warm spot in my heart for Canada." Over the next 36 years, the Bells would live in both Washington, DC, and Nova Scotia.

But Beinn Bhreagh would become much more than a summer vacation spot for the Bells. They built a large home there along with laboratories, work sheds, hangars, and barns. The estate was a place where Alexander had no obligations. The wide-open spaces and brisk seaside winds were perfect for the last great idea Bell had up his sleeve, one he'd dreamed about since boyhood: a flying machine.

FLYING MEN

FLIGHT HAD long fascinated Bell. As a boy in Edinburgh he would climb to the top of hills to be closer to the birds that soared overhead. Thomas Watson wrote that Bell had begun pondering human flight long before inventing the telephone, discussing "the possibility of making a machine that would fly like a bird" with his partner and friend. The inventor was convinced that a flying machine was doable. Bell even asked Watson in 1877 to promise he'd start experiments in flight with him "as soon as the telephone business became established, if it ever did."

By the 1890s, Bell had the time, money, and space to take up his postponed study of flying.

When a magazine reporter in 1893 asked him what society's next great invention would be, Bell commented that the ability to travel by flying machine would bring a "revolution in the world's methods of transportation and making war." He told the reporter, "I have not the shadow of a doubt that the problem of aerial navigation will be solved within ten years." This was a shocking thing to say back then. Most scientists of the day didn't believe that human flight was possible. At least not the **heavier-than-air** kind of flight, like airplanes and helicopters.

People had been flying in **lighter-than-air** balloons since the 1780s. But going from the ground up into the air as birds did was different. It required complicated engines and the control of unseen forces. The "birdmen" who strapped on giant wings, harnessed themselves into hang gliders, or climbed into smoke-spewing flying contraptions weren't seen as serious scientists. They were thought to be cranks and crazies, fools and showmen.

But that was changing thanks to Otto Lilienthal. The German glider expert took a scientific approach to flight experiments. Like today's hang gliders, Lilienthal launched himself from hilltops while attached to sail-like wings. But unlike many flying men before him, Lilienthal documented and repeated his successful glider flights and wrote scientific papers about his observations and experiments.

Bell read Lilienthal's papers, as did one of the most famous scientists of the time, Samuel Langley, the head of the Smithsonian Institution in Washington, DC. Langley and Bell knew each other, were scientific colleagues, and shared a passion for the pursuit of human flight.

Langley experimented by flying models. His small flyers had spinning propellers powered by twisted rubber (somewhat like rubber band–powered toy airplanes). He tested different kinds of wings and propellers. By the time he showed some to Bell in 1891, he'd tried dozens. Alexander wrote to Mabel, "Langley's flying machines—They flew for me today. I shall have to make experiments upon my own account in Cape Breton. Can't keep out of it. It will be all UP with us someday!"

By 1895, Langley had a large 14-foot (4-m) model airplane powered by a small steam engine. He called it an **aerodrome**, which means "air runner" in Greek. "I must confess that it was a rather startling experience actually to see a steam engine flying in the air like a bird," Alexander wrote Mabel. "I shall count this day as one of the more memorable of my life." The following year, on May 6, 1896, Langley provided an even more memorable demonstration.

Bell himself took this photograph of Langley's model aerodrome flying over the Potomac River in May 1896. *Aërial Locomotion: With a Few Notes of Progress in the Construction of an Aërodrome* by Alexander Graham Bell and Cyrus Adler

Many people still thought flying was for silly fools, not scientists, so Langley didn't want to try out his newest aerodrome in public and risk being ridiculed. He'd purchased a houseboat for launching the aerodromes by catapult out over a shallow section of the nearby Potomac River. Langley invited only his trusted friend Bell to be a witness. Wanting to get the best view, Bell took a rowboat out into the river. He also brought a camera. "It resembled an enormous bird, soaring in the air…sweeping steadily upward in a spiral path," Bell wrote in a letter to *Science* magazine. Langley's aerodrome flew about a half mile (0.8 km)and made two flights. "No one could have witnessed these experiments without being convinced that the practicability of mechanical flight had been demonstrated."

Samuel Langley

Samuel Pierpont Langley was an **astronomer**, physicist, and inventor. Like Bell, Langley was a self-taught scientist. Neither man graduated from a university, and both learned much of what they knew from studying books. Langley invented the bolometer, an instrument that measures solar radiation, in 1880. He became secretary of the Smithsonian Institution in 1887. Under his leadership there, both the National Zoo and Astrophysical Observatory were created. His pioneering work in the study of flight, or **aeronautics**, made him famous. Langley Air Force Base in Virginia and NASA's Langley Research Center are named for him.

The successful aerodrome flights witnessed by Bell in 1896 got the attention of the US government. The War Department granted Langley $50,000 to build an aerodrome large enough to carry a pilot. The Smithsonian funded him with an additional $20,000. The money supported a workshop of carpenters, engine makers, and machine workers, and by the autumn of 1903 his *Great Aerodrome* was ready.

On October 7, 1903, test pilot Charles Manly climbed into the aircraft and was catapulted down a track mounted on a houseboat. Manly and the *Great Aerodrome* tumbled off the boat and into the Potomac River. Langley tried again on December 8 with the same result. Nine days later, the Wright brothers flew the first powered, heavier-than-air machine at Kitty Hawk, North Carolina.

In 1914—after Langley's death—the Smithsonian paid Glenn Curtiss to rebuild and fly the *Great Aerodrome*. After modifying the aerodrome and replacing its engine, Curtiss was able to make a few brief hops into the air. The Smithsonian Institution put Langley's aerodrome on display with the sign: THE FIRST MAN-CARRYING AEROPLANE IN THE HISTORY OF THE WORLD CAPABLE OF SUSTAINED FREE FLIGHT. The display stayed that way until 1942 when, as Orville Wright had been asking for decades, the Smithsonian admitted that the original aerodrome could not have flown as it had been in 1903.

Uplifting Experiments

Many early experimenters in human flight paid a high price. Just months after witnessing the flight of Langley's steam-powered aerodrome, Otto Lilienthal died in a glider accident. "A dead man tells no tales," Bell noted. "He advances no further and his death acts as a deterrent upon others.... How can ideas be tested without actually going into the air and risking one's life on what might be an erroneous judgment?" Flying was dangerous business.

Bell wisely started his study of human flight from the safety of the ground. "I have been continuously at work upon experiments relating to kites," he wrote, "because of the intimate connection of the subject with the flying machine problem." His plan was to design a kite that could safely lift a person; once that was perfected, he would then add an engine to it. "If a kite flies well... when loaded with the equivalent to a man and motor, then if provided with an engine, it should travel through the air," he wrote. It was a similar plan that

Bell (far right) and his assistants flying a giant ring kite. Library of Congress, LC-G9-Z1-116,451-A

two bicycle-making brothers named Wright were using, too.

Soon kites of all sizes and shapes soared above Beinn Bhreagh. Some of the locals thought their famous neighbor was crazy to spend his days flying kites. "He goes up there on the side of the hill on sunny afternoons and with a lot of thing-ma-jigs, fools away the whole blessed day, flying kites, mind you," local boatman John Hamilton Parkin recounted of an observer's comment. "He sets up a blackboard and puts down figures about these kites and queer machines he keeps bobbing around in the sky. Dozens of them he has.... It's the greatest foolishness I ever did see."

Even Helen Keller thought her friend a bit obsessed after a visit in 1901. "Mr. Bell has nothing but kites and flying-machines on his tongue's end," she wrote. But flying the big kites was quite memorable to the young woman. One day, Keller told Bell that the strings he would be using for a particular large kite seemed too weak. Bell didn't agree and sent the kite up anyway. "It began to pull and tug, and lo, the wires broke, and off went the [kite]," wrote Keller. "After that he asked me if the strings were all right and changed them at once when I answered in the negative. Altogether we had great fun."

Kite flying was a family activity at Beinn Bhreagh for many years. The boy in front of Bell is his grandson. Library of Congress, LC-G9-Z3-116,837-AB

TRIANGLE POWER

THE SKIES above Bell's kite field were filled with box kites covered in red silk, white ring-shaped kites, cylindrical spool kites, and even star-shaped kites. But Bell soon found his favorite kite shape: a tetrahedron. A tetrahedron is a four-sided object whose sides and base are all triangles. Its design makes a lightweight but strong kite.

"I believe [the tetrahedron] will prove of importance not only in kite architecture," Bell wrote, "but in forming all sorts of skeleton frameworks for all sorts of constructing." Tetrahedral arches and supports would also work for bridges and to hold up heavy ceilings, he reasoned.

Bell put his beloved tetrahedron to work in kite construction. In 1905, he assembled 1,300 silk-covered wood tetrahedral cells into a massive kite called the *Frost King*. The kite looked like a flying piece of giant honeycomb. One worker was unexpectedly lifted 40 feet (12 m) into the air when he held on to the *Frost King* too long! But the incident proved that Bell's tetrahedral kite design had the power to carry humans into the air. Could it also carry an engine and be steered? Could Bell's design be made into a flying machine?

Daughter Marian shares a kiss with Alexander surrounded by one of his tetrahedral kite frames. Library of Congress, LC-DIG-ds-06863

PYRAMID POWER

How powerful are triangles? Compare a cube and a tetrahedron to find out.

You'll Need

- Printouts of the cube and tetrahedron patterns
- Pen or pencil
- Card stock or file folder
- Scissors
- Tape
- 2 raw eggs
- Paper towels or newspaper
- Yardstick

1. Use a photocopier or computer to enlarge the cube and tetrahedron patterns. Make sure to keep both patterns the same relative size. (If you enlarge the cube 150 percent, then do the same for the tetrahedron.) You can also use graph paper to trace and enlarge them.

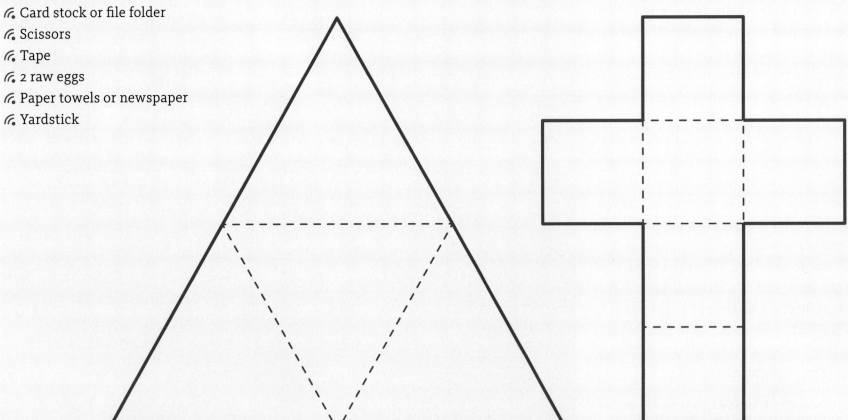

2. Use each pattern to cut out the two shapes in card stock. Score along the dashed lines using a sharp pencil, so you'll know where the fold lines are. Then remove the patterns.

3. Fold each shape at the score lines. Use tape to close up the shapes, leaving a single flap open. In other words, apply tape to only one edge of the tetrahedron but to four edges of the cube. Use just enough tape to hold the sides together. Ideally, you'll end up with equal amounts of tape on each shape to keep their weight equal.

4. Place an egg inside each shape and close them up with tape. Again, don't use much tape. You'll need to be able to peek inside.

5. Put some newspaper or paper towels on the floor. Set the yardstick nearby. Ready for the test?

6. Hold the cube so its bottom is parallel to the floor. Raise it up so the bottom is 2 inches (5 cm) above the floor and let it go. Any cracks in the egg? Do the same with the tetrahedron, holding its flat bottom parallel to the floor and releasing it from a 2-inch (5-cm) height. Did it crack?

7. Repeat step 6 holding each shape so a corner is 2 inches (5 cm) from the floor. Different results?

8. Keep repeating steps 6 and 7, increasing the height until an egg breaks. Which shape won the strength test?

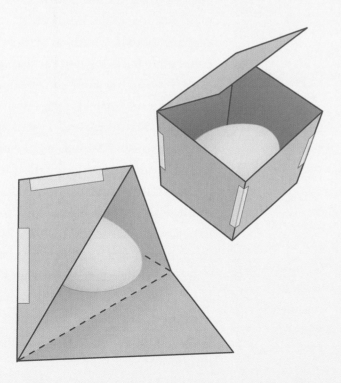

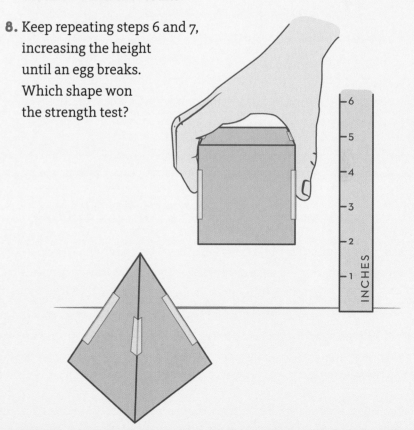

101

The Wright Brothers

Wilbur and Orville Wright were brothers and bicycle makers from Dayton, Ohio. Like Alexander Graham Bell and Samuel Langley, the brothers followed Otto Lilienthal's gliding experiments and read his writings. The Wrights experimented with human-controlled gliders, too. Once they'd designed a glider that could be controlled by its pilot through wing warping, the brothers developed propellers and an engine to power their flyer. They achieved the first powered, sustained, and controlled airplane flight in their *Wright Flyer* on December 17, 1903, near Kitty Hawk, North Carolina. In 1905, they built and flew the first fully practical airplane, which could turn, circle, and fly for more than half an hour.

The Wrights and Bell's Aerial Experiment Association (AEA) were competitors. The company that Glenn Curtiss later created was sued by the Wrights for infringing on their patent. Curtiss also joined with the Smithsonian to cast doubt on the Wrights' legacy of being the first in flight. Today the original *Wright Flyer* is displayed in the Smithsonian Air and Space Museum with a plaque saying: THE WORLD'S FIRST POWER-DRIVEN HEAVIER-THAN-AIR MACHINE.

Glenn Curtiss

Glenn Hammond Curtiss was a motorcycle builder, champion motorcycle racer, and lightweight engine expert when he joined Bell's AEA. After the success of the *June Bug* airplane, Curtiss started his own aircraft company. In 1911, he built the first practical seaplane. The Curtiss Aeroplane and Motor Company received the first contract to build airplanes for the US Navy and built 5,000 biplanes for World War I. His best-known plane was the JN-4, or "Jenny," a training airplane widely used in World War I and later by barnstormers, or stunt pilots.

AERIAL EXPERIMENTS

BY THE time the *Frost King* flew, the race to build the first flying machine was already won. Orville and Wilbur Wright flew the world's first airplane in late 1903. And by 1905, the Wrights had an airplane that could stay in the air for more than 30 minutes. But aeronautics was a young science with lots of room for improvement. Bell believed that aerodromes, as he and Samuel Langley called airplanes, needed to be safer. How? Being more stable and therefore less likely to tip would help. But besides experimenting with ways to make airplanes more stable, Bell wanted to design an aerodrome that wouldn't crash-land, one that could glide back down to earth and safely land even if its engine stopped working.

Getting new projects off the ground takes money. Great ideas and lots of enthusiasm aren't enough. Mabel proposed that her husband form an organization to more easily attract the funding he needed to experiment with human flight. And so the Aerial Experiment Association (AEA) was born in 1907. It included engineers Frederick Walker "Casey" Baldwin and John Alexander Douglas McCurdy, the son of the newspaperman with the faulty phone; motorcycle racer and engine builder Glenn Curtiss; and US Army lieutenant Thomas Selfridge. Mabel personally funded the AEA, becoming one of

BUILD A TETRAHEDRAL KITE

Find out why Bell was so fascinated by kites and tetrahedrons by making your own tetrahedral kite.

   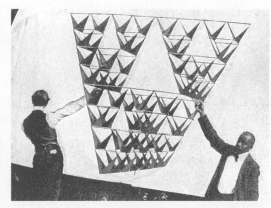

Each single tetrahedral cell (far left) is combined with others to build a kite. *Popular Science Monthly*, December 1903

You'll Need

🎼 Ruler or yardstick

🎼 Kite string

🎼 Scissors

🎼 24 thin, lightweight plastic drinking straws or coffee stirrers

🎼 Sheet of paper

🎼 Marker

🎼 4 sheets of tissue paper

🎼 Glue stick

1. Cut a piece of kite string about 3 feet (1 m) long. Thread the string through five straws, like beads on a chain. Leave a good amount of loose string on both ends.

2. Arrange the five straws on the string, as shown, so they form a split-diamond shape.

Continued on next page...

3. Tie each of the loose string ends to the corner string that runs between adjacent straws. Pull the string tight, and make triple knots. The straws of the tied-up split-diamond shape need to be touching, as shown.

4. Cut a length of string twice as long as a straw. Thread a sixth straw onto it, and then tie it to one of the diamond's outer corners that has no knots, as shown. Tie it tight and triple knot it.

5. Lift up the single straw and the corner opposite it and loop the end of the single straw's string around the corner. Tie the two together tightly and triple knot it. You have a tetrahedron!

6. Repeat steps 1 through 3 another three times to complete four six-straw tetrahedrons.

7. Set one of your tetrahedrons on a sheet of regular paper. Use the marker to trace around the base triangle. Keeping the tetrahedron in the same spot, tip it over and trace the outside of that side, as shown.

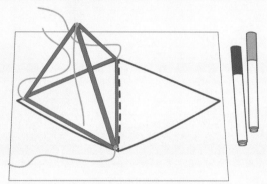

8. Remove the straw tetrahedron and sketch in some flaps, as shown. The fatter your straw, the wider the flaps should be. Now you have a tissue paper template!

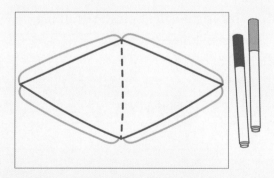

9. Use the template to cut out a total of four tissue paper sails. Cut all around the template, including the flaps. You can cut them all out at the same time if you stack up four layers of tissue paper before cutting.

10. Attach the tissue paper sails to the straw tetrahedrons. Spread glue on both flaps of one side of the sail and fold the flaps up and over the straws.

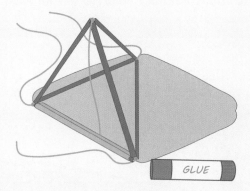

11. Then tip the tetrahedron over and glue the opposite two flaps onto the straws, so that two sides of the shape are covered by the paper sail. This is one tetrahedral kite cell.

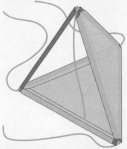

12. Finish gluing all four kite cells and let them dry. Then set one of the cells above two others to make a big triangle, as shown. All three of the tissue-paper sails need to face the same direction. Use all the dangling string ends to tie the three cells together tightly.

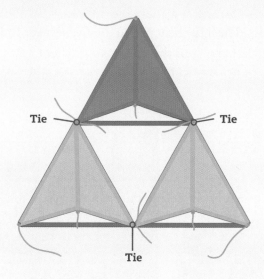

13. Set the fourth tetrahedron on top of the others and tie it on so it makes a pyramid. Trim off all the string tails. Tie the spool of kite string onto the very top of the pyramid, as shown.

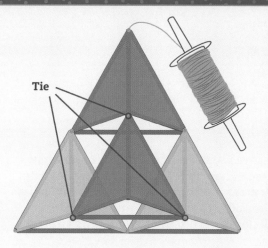

14. Get flying! A day with some wind works best because of the kite's weight. A running start helps, too. Pull the kite so the wind goes inside the sails. If your kite flies erratically, a tail might help. Attach it to the bottom of the pyramid, opposite of where you attached the lead.

the first women to give money to a research organization.

The AEA's first project was getting one of Bell's kites into the air—with a person on it. The *Cygnet* was his biggest kite ever. It was made of more than 3,300 red silk tetrahedral cells. The kite was attached to floating pontoons, and the whole thing was towed by a powerful boat. On December 6, 1907, Selfridge lay down inside a flat section of the huge kite. The large boat pulled the *Cygnet* over Bras d'Or Lake, and the kite rose 104 feet (32 m) into the air. Selfridge hovered steadily over-head in the kite for seven long minutes. When the wind died down, the *Cygnet* gracefully descended toward the water. Someone was supposed to cut the rope connecting the kite and boat as soon as the *Cygnet* touched down. But Selfridge couldn't see out of the kite very well, and a puff of smoke from the boat's engine clouded the view. No one saw the kite's pontoons hit the water, so the rope wasn't cut in time. The speeding boat instantly jerked the delicate kite forward, dragging it through the lake and ripping it to pieces. Selfridge had to be rescued from the freezing water.

BELOW: Members of the Aerial Experiment Association: (left to right) "Casey" Baldwin, Lieutenant Thomas Selfridge, Glenn Curtiss, Alexander Graham Bell, and Douglas McCurdy next to their *White Wing* airplane.
Courtesy City of Vancouver Archives, CVA 371-2326

RIGHT: Bell (far right) stands on the dock as the *Cygnet* is towed from its storage shed.
Library of Congress, LC-G9-Z1-139,226-A

The AEA decided it was time to try flying something besides kites. They turned their attention to biplanes—airplanes with two stacked wings. This shape was working for the Wright brothers. Selfridge designed the *Red Wing* biplane complete with an engine. Baldwin piloted the airplane with red silk–covered wings on a short 100-yard (92-m) flight. But on a second flight it tipped sideways and crashed. Bell quickly figured out why. The airplane needed movable wing flaps, called **ailerons**, to give the craft stability.

The AEA's next aircraft, the *White Wing*, became the first airplane with ailerons in North America. It also had a three-wheeled undercarriage to make takeoff and landing easier. Baldwin designed this AEA airplane, and he, Selfridge, Curtiss, and McCurdy flew it in May 1908 until it crashed when caught in a wind gust.

The AEA's third craft was designed and flown by Curtiss. The AEA entered the *June Bug* in a competition on July 4, 1908—and won. The contest, sponsored by *Scientific American*, was for the first public flight over a kilometer-long course. The *June Bug* not only won but also went on to fly 150 more times without crashing. "Hurrah for Curtiss! Hurrah for the June Bug! Hurrah for the Aerial Association!" telegrammed Bell to his team.

The award-winning flight of the AEA's *June Bug* airplane piloted by Glenn Curtiss on July 4, 1908. Library of Congress, LC-USZ62-59026

A Historic Tragedy

Rescuers tend to wounded pilot Orville Wright and passenger Lieutenant Selfridge near the crumpled *Wright Flyer*.
Library of Congress, LC-DIG-ds-01202

SELFRIDGE, McCURDY, Curtiss, and Baldwin relaxed at Beinn Bhreagh as well as worked. The young men spent time telling stories, playing billiards, and fencing. Bell's grandson Melville Grosvenor remembered how much fun it was as a boy to watch the test flights in a nearby field, after which "we drove home at night under the stars, Grampy and the AEA boys singing all the way." The four men were like adopted sons of the Bells, so news of an accident involving one of them hit the family hard.

In September 1908, the Wright brothers were demonstrating their airplane, the *Wright Flyer*, on two continents. Wilbur Wright was in France, stunning crowds by flying figure eights in the sky. Outside of Washington, DC, Orville Wright was demonstrating their airplane for the military. The Wrights were hoping to sell their airplane to the US Army Signal Corps. (There was no US Air Force yet.)

The *Wright Flyer* had a passenger seat and a pilot seat. That meant Orville could take people on flights and give them a firsthand flying experience. The most important passengers were military officers interested in knowing if the airplane would be useful to the army. Orville knew that Lieutenant Selfridge was part of the AEA. Hadn't everyone heard about the *June Bug*'s flights earlier that year? Wright suspected that Selfridge was really at the demonstrations to spy on the competition. But he agreed to let the army lieutenant be a passenger on September 17.

Wright and Selfridge took off and made three smooth circles above Fort Myer. Then Wright heard a tapping sound over the noisy

engine, followed by two loud thuds. One of the propellers had broken off and been flung into the rudder of the *Wright Flyer*. "Quick as a flash, the machine turned down in front and started straight for the ground," recalled Wright. The fragile airplane made of wood and canvas plunged into the dirt. The engine was torn loose, and both pilot and passenger were pinned under a wing. Rescuers ran toward the crumpled airplane and dragged the unconscious Lieutenant Selfridge from the wreckage. His skull had been badly fractured. Selfridge died later that day while in

surgery. He was the first person to die in an airplane crash.

"Let's hold tight together, all the tighter for the one that's gone," Mabel wrote to her husband upon learning of Selfridge's death. The other AEA members decided to go ahead and finish up their last airplane in his honor. It was McCurdy who designed the fourth and final AEA airplane, the *Silver Dart*. On February 23, 1909, native Canadian McCurdy piloted his fragile airplane off the ice of Bras d'Or Lake and flew a short half-mile (0.8-km) flight. It was Canads's first-ever airplane flight.

LEFT: The AEA's *Silver Dart* airplane flying over the frozen Bras d'Or Lake of Cape Breton Island.
Library of Congress, LC-G9-Z1-130,728-A

ABOVE: Douglas McCurdy poses in the crude cockpit of the AEA's *Silver Dart* airplane.
Courtesy City of Toronto Archives, Fonds 1244, Item 79

Controlling Flight

The Wright brothers were first in flight because they understood that controlling an airplane presented a brand-new problem. Unlike other kinds of vehicles, an airplane moves freely in three dimensions. Powered flight has three axes of movement: **yaw**, **pitch**, and **roll**.

Getting a machine off the ground and into the air isn't enough. An airplane is stable only when controlled in all three dimensions. Like a car or boat, an airplane can move right to left. This is yaw and is controlled by a fin called a rudder. Like a submarine or balloon, an airplane can move up and down. This is pitch, and it is controlled by an elevator. But unlike cars, boats, submarines, or balloons, airplanes also tip side to side. This is called roll. Figuring out how to control roll was the key to controlling flight.

The Wrights controlled roll in their first airplanes with a system of cables that pulled on the two stacked flexible wings, like twisting an empty toothpaste box. Changing the shape of the canvas-covered wooden wings controlled how far and to which side their airplane rolled. This twisting was called wing warping. Ailerons replaced wing warping. The wing flaps accomplished the same control without needing to twist the entire wing system. Ailerons allowed airplanes to be single-winged and built of sturdier, nonflexible materials like aluminum.

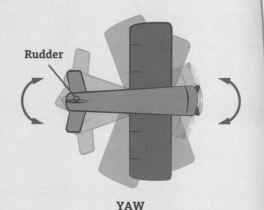

Rudder

YAW

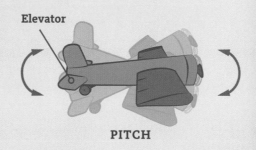

Elevator

PITCH

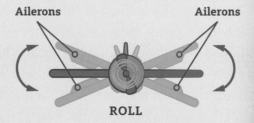

Ailerons   **Ailerons**

ROLL

An Inventor to the Very End

"Mr. Watson, come here. I need you," spoke an aging Bell into a duplicate of his 40-year-old Centennial Telephone. "It would take me a week to get to you this time," Watson replied with a smile. Bell was in New York City and Watson in San Francisco that afternoon of January 25, 1915. The two famous men were making a ceremonial telephone call to celebrate the first telephone line to cross the North American continent.

"The telephone has gone all over the world.... It has grown far beyond my knowledge," Bell admitted in a speech. "The telephone system as we now know it is the product of many, many minds, to whom honor should be given for the wonderful and beneficial work it has accomplished. I can only say that I am proud and thankful of the fact that it was my crude telephone of 1874–75 that originated the great industry that we see today." Who can imagine a world without telephones and all the inventions inspired by it—fax machines, scanners, mobile phones, internet modems, and smartphones?

Bell was always a progressive thinker ahead of his time. He supported women's rights. On his 66th birthday, he and Mabel cheered at a Washington, DC, march for women's voting rights. He believed in civil rights for all people and spoke out against the suffocating racism that was commonplace during his lifetime.

He never slowed down or stopped experimenting and inventing, either. In a speech he gave in 1891, he explained, "[The inventor] is haunted by an idea. The spirit of invention possesses him, seeking materialization." And so it was with Bell. His inventions transmitted sounds and combated sickness. His constructions soared through the air and towered over the land. There was only one final element left for Bell to tame: water.

FLYING OVER WATER

AFTER THE AEA quit flying, the Bells took a round-the-world tour with Casey Baldwin and his wife, Kathleen. While in Italy, the two men met with Enrico Forlanini, the inventor of the **hydrofoil**. It wasn't a visit they'd soon forget! Forlanini took Bell and Baldwin out on his hydrofoil boat. The men sped "over Lake Maggiore at express train speed," wrote Mabel. Casey declared that the high-speed ride was as smooth as flying.

Bell and Baldwin had tinkered with their own hydrofoil designs and model boats back in Nova Scotia. Bell preferred to call the boats **hydrodromes**, which means "water runners." The term related the watercraft to aerodromes, what Bell still insisted on calling airplanes. Bell's Italian boat ride revived the inventor's

Bell's HD-4 hydrofoil. Wikimedia Commons

········ The Hydrofoil ········

A hydrofoil is a boat that lifts its hull above the surface of the water when traveling at high speeds. A hydrofoil has wings, called foils, that stay underwater. The foils work like airplane wings: as water rushes past them, they lift the boat out of the water. Hydrofoils also ride smoothly in rough water because the foils reduce the effects of waves.

Italian engineer Enrico Forlanini invented the hydrofoil around 1900. In 1906, he successfully tested the first full-size, self-propelled hydrofoil. Today, commercial hydrofoils carry hundreds of thousands of passengers and many tons of supplies and equipment each year. The military also uses high-speed hydrofoils.

THE AIM OF AILERONS

See the difference that ailerons make in controlling flight! Build a glider and then fly it with and without ailerons.

You'll Need

- Tracing paper
- Pen or pencil
- Scissors
- Card stock or file folder
- Drinking straw
- Ruler
- Tape
- Paper clips

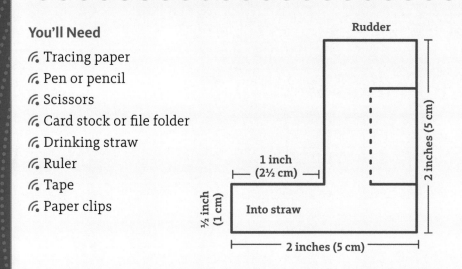

Rudder

1 inch
(2½ cm)

½ inch
(1 cm)

Into straw

2 inches (5 cm)

2 inches (5 cm)

1. Trace the rudder pattern and use it to cut a rudder out from card stock or a file folder. Cut the two short solid lines on the pattern and fold along the dashed line. Slip the rudder into the straw, as shown.

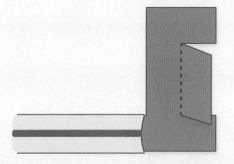

2. Use a ruler to draw a 2-by-4-inch (5-by-10-cm) rectangle on card stock and cut it out. Mark the center with a pen or pencil. Tape the rectangle to the tail of the glider, as shown, using the center mark to line it up under the straw. The rudder end should be flush with the card tail.

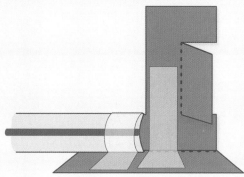

3. Use a ruler to draw a 2-by-8-inch (5-by-20-cm) rectangle on card stock and cut it out. This is your wing. Mark the center of the wing with a dashed line; also mark dashed lines 1 inch (2½ cm) in from both ends. Crease and fold all three lines.

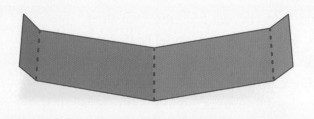

4. Slip a couple of paperclips onto the front of the straw for weight. Then find the balance point on the straw fuselage by setting it on top of a bottle or finger and moving it around until it balances. Use a pen to mark the balance point. Then tape the center of the wing to the balance point on the straw.

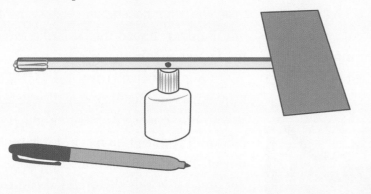

5. Cut some short slits on the back edge of the tail and bend the flaps to create elevators, as shown. These will control the up-and-down pitch of your glider.

6. Give it a toss! You can adjust the elevator and rudder flaps to improve the glider. How does it fly?

7. Now add ailerons by cutting some slits on each side of the back edge of your wing. These will control the roll of your glider.

8. Fly the glider again, adjusting the aileron, elevator, and rudder flaps to improve its flight. Adding another paperclip might help, too. Do the ailerons make a difference? How?

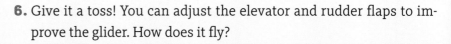

Ailerons

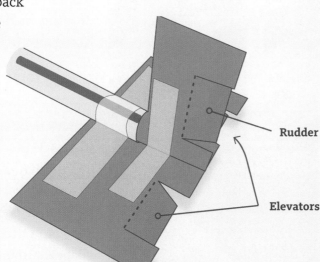

Rudder

Elevators

enthusiasm for hydrofoil design. Once back at Beinn Bhreagh, he and Baldwin began building their own boats that flew on water. They ended up creating the fastest hydrofoil in the world.

The pair named their hydrofoil the HD, an abbreviation of *hydrodrome*. Their first full-size hydrofoil, the HD-1, reached a respectable speed of 30 mph (48 kph). By the third model, the HD-3, the boat was streaking across Baddeck Bay at 50 mph (80 kph). By 1919, Baldwin and Bell had built a huge,

Bell with engineer Casey Baldwin and his son in hydrofoil HD-4 in 1919.
Library of Congress, LC-G9-Z1-155,834-A

streamlined hydrofoil called the HD-4. This sleek, 60-foot (18-m) long boat was shaped like a torpedo with wings. The US Navy had passed on buying Bell's HD design a few years earlier. But with World War I over, the navy reconsidered and sent Bell two of its big engines to test. These 350-horsepower engines powered two above-water aerial propellers that boosted the boat's speed. Bell and Baldwin hoped they'd make the HD-4 the fastest boat in the world.

On September 9, 1919, the HD-4 began moving across Baddeck Bay. It was another ride to remember. "At fifteen knots [17 mph (28 kph)] you feel the machine rising bodily out of the water, and once up and clear of the **drag** [of water] she drives ahead with an acceleration that makes you grip your seat to keep from being left behind," wrote William Nutting in the *Motor Boat* magazine after going for a ride. "The wind on your face is like the pressure of a giant hand and an occasional dash of fine spray stings like birdshot.... It's unbelievable—it defies the laws of physics, but it's true."

The HD-4 set a world's marine speed record that day when it flew atop the water at an unbelievable 70.86 mph (114 kph). But Bell never personally rode in the HD-4. He just didn't feel up to it. He suffered from **diabetes**, and the disease was weakening his health.

Mabel and Alexander enjoyed each other's company through 45 years of marriage. Wikimedia Commons

A 1915 AT&T advertisement with the caption, MAKING A NEIGHBORHOOD OF A NATION: THE TRANSCONTINENTAL TELEPHONE LINE. Wikimedia Commons

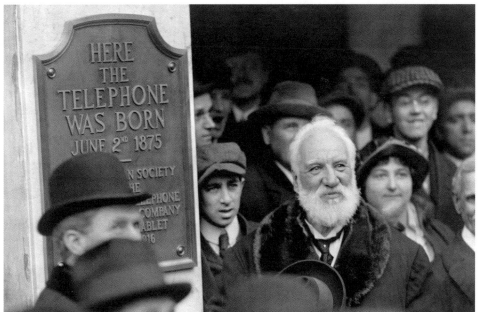

Bell at an unveiling of a plaque in Boston that commemorates the 40th anniversary of the invention of the telephone. Library of Congress, LC-USZ62-117582

LIFE AND LEGACY

BY LATE July 1922, Bell was seriously ill. He died on August 2, at age 75. Mabel was at her husband's side when he passed away at his beloved Beinn Bhreagh estate.

The inventor was laid in a simple pine coffin, made by his workmen and lined with leftover kite fabric. A large rock serves as the grave marker of Alexander and Mabel, who died only five months later. Under Alexander Graham Bell's name, it reads simply: INVENTOR • TEACHER. At the time of Bell's burial, all telephone service in Canada and the United States was stopped for one minute in honor of the inventor.

In a graduation speech near the end of his life, Bell talked about his life of discovery and invention. He encouraged the graduates to find their own true lives, to not simply follow the easiest path. "Leave the beaten track occasionally and dive into the woods," he urged. "Every time you do so you will be certain to find something you have never seen before. Of course it will be a little thing, but do not ignore it. Follow it up, explore all round it; one discovery will lead to another, and before you know it you will have something worth thinking about to occupy your mind. All really big discoveries are the results of thought."

LEFT: Bell and his three granddaughters enjoying Beinn Bhreagh. Library of Congress, LC-G9-Z1-116,785-A

RIGHT: "All really big discoveries are the results of thought," said Alexander Graham Bell. Library of Congress, LC-USZ62-92864

Resources

Want to find out more about Alexander Graham Bell, his inventions and experiments, as well as his work with the hearing impaired? Check out these books, websites, and places to visit.

BOOKS TO READ

Books with 🎧 are targeted to young readers and/or are highly illustrated.

🎧 Bader, Bonnie. *Who Was Alexander Graham Bell?* New York: Grosset and Dunlap, 2013.

🎧 Cunningham, Kevin. *Cell Phones.* North Mankato, MN: Cherry Lake, 2007.

🎧 DK Editors. *The First Telephone.* New York: DK Children, 2015.

🎧 Fandel, Jennifer. *Alexander Graham Bell and the Telephone.* North Mankato, MN: Capstone, 2006.

🎧 Grant, Reg. *Flight: 100 Years of Aviation.* New York: DK, 2010.

Gray, Charlotte. *Reluctant Genius: The Passionate Life and Inventive Mind of Alexander Graham Bell.* Toronto, ON: Phyllis Bruce/Harper-Collins, 2006.

🎧 Grosvenor, Edwin S., and Morgan Wesson. *Alexander Graham Bell: The Life and Times of the Man Who Invented the Telephone.* New York: Harry N. Abrams, 1997.

🎧 Honovich, Nancy. *Alexander Graham Bell.* San Diego: Silver Dolphin Books, 2009.

Keller, Helen. *The Story of My Life.* New York: Doubleday, 1903.

🎧 Matthews, Tom. *Always Inventing: A Photobiography of Alexander Graham Bell.* Washington, DC: National Geographic Children's Books, 2015.

Shulman, Seth. *The Telephone Gambit: Chasing Alexander Graham Bell's Secret.* New York: W. W. Norton, 2008.

🎧 Spilsbury, Louise. *Alexander Graham Bell and the Telephone.* New York: PowerKids, 2016.

Watson, Thomas A. *Exploring Life: The Autobiography of Thomas A. Watson.* New York: Appleton, 1926.

PLACES TO VISIT IN PERSON OR ONLINE

Alexander Graham Bell National Historic Site

559 Chebucto Street
Baddeck, Nova Scotia
Canada
(902) 295-2069
www.pc.gc.ca/en/lhn-nhs/ns/grahambell

This Parks Canada National Historic Site is situated on 25 acres of land with a view of the Bras d'Or Lake in Baddeck on Cape Breton Island, Nova Scotia. The Bells' Beinn Bhreagh estate is viewable from the grounds. The onsite museum features artifacts donated by the Bell family, a full-scale replica of the hydrofoil boat that set the world speed record in 1919, the original HD-4 hull, and a replica of the AEA *Silver Dart* piloted in 1909 by Douglas McCurdy. There are also exhibits about Bell's many years of research into the transmission of speech and sound by both electric wire and sunlight, his endeavors with kites, and displays explaining his work with people who were deaf.

Bell Homestead National Historic Site

94 Tutela Heights Road
Brantford, Ontario
Canada
(519) 756-6220
www.bellhomestead.ca

Visitors can tour the home of Alexander Graham Bell's parents, view a collection of historic artifacts, observe staff in period costumes going about household chores, and visit the Grand River overlook site where a young Bell dreamed of inventing the telephone.

Library of Congress

10 First Street SE
Washington, DC 20540
(202) 707-8000
www.loc.gov

You can visit and tour the Library of Congress in Washington, DC, as well as do research in the reading rooms there. Information on visiting as well as virtual tours of all three buildings are online at www.loc.gov/visit. Tens of thousands of scanned images and documents about Alexander Graham Bell are archived at the library. There are photographs, personal letters, laboratory notebooks, invention blueprints, journals, and more available for viewing online from these collections:
Alexander Graham Bell Family Papers: www.loc.gov/collections/alexander-graham-bell-papers/
Gilbert H. Grosvenor Collection of Photographs of the Alexander Graham Bell Family: www.loc.gov/pictures/item/2004681412/

The National Museum of American History

Smithsonian Institution
14th Street and Constitution Avenue, NW
Washington, DC 20001
(202) 633-1000
http://americanhistory.si.edu

You can see two 1876 telephones built and used by Alexander Graham Bell at the Smithsonian's National Museum of American History. On display in the *American Stories* exhibit is one of the two telephones he used in public demonstrations in 1876, and the *American Enterprise* exhibit displays an electromagnetic telephone that Bell showcased at the Philadelphia Centennial Exhibition in 1876. The museum has ongoing Inventing in America exhibits in collaboration with the US Patent and Trademark Office, too. The museum's website features lots of information on Alexander Graham Bell's inventions and his work at the Volta Lab in Washington, DC, during the 1880s. You can even hear a test recording of his voice recovered from a flat wax disc. Hear My Voice: Alexander Graham Bell and the Origins of Recorded Sound: http://americanhistory.si.edu/exhibitions/hear-my-voice

National Air and Space Museum

Smithsonian Institution
Independence Ave at 6th Street, SW
Washington, DC 20560
(202) 633-2214
https://airandspace.si.edu

The Early Flight gallery at the National Air and Space Museum tells the story of early airplane development, including the contributions of Samuel P. Langley and members of Alexander Graham Bell's AEA. Langley's Aerodrome #5, the unpiloted steam-engine aircraft that Bell excitedly witnessed flying in 1896, hangs in the gallery. So does a quarter-scale model of Langley's unsuccessful Great Aerodrome (the one that dumped its pilot into the Potomac River twice in 1903). There is a 1909 Wright Military Flyer on display, too, the world's first military airplane. This is the aircraft that crashed in 1908, killing AEA member Lt. Thomas E. Selfridge. An airplane built by AEA member Glenn Curtiss's company, the Curtiss Model D "Headless Pusher," is also featured.

Museum of Communications

7000 East Marginal Way South
Seattle, Washington 98108
(206) 767-3012
www.museumofcommunications.org

The museum displays many telephones from the past to the present, including an exact replica of Alexander Graham Bell's 1876 telephone. That's the one into which he spoke the famous words "Mr. Watson—Come here—I want to see you."

Telecommunications History Group

1425 Champa Street
Denver, Colorado 80202
(303) 296-1221
www.telcomhistory.org

The museum gives tours on Wednesdays or by appointment. The website has a terrific Virtual Museum with exhibits like *The Science of Phones* as well as a tour of their archive.

National Inventors Hall of Fame Museum

600 Dulany Street
Alexandria, Virginia 22314
(571) 272-0095
www.invent.org/honor/hall-of-fame-museum/

Find out about inventors past and present by exploring the lives and stories of the inventions of more than 530 National Inventors Hall of Fame Inductees through interactive kiosks and exhibits.

Roseville Telephone Museum

106 Vernon Street
Roseville, California 95678
www.consolidated.com/about-us/history/telephone-museum/

This 4,500-square-foot museum houses one of the most extensive collections of antique telephones in the nation.

New Hampshire Telephone Museum

One Depot Street
Warner, New Hampshire 03278
(603) 456-2234
http://nhtelephonemuseum.com

Both guided and self-guided app tours enlighten visitors about the important moments in telephone history and feature more than 1,000 artifacts. Did you know that the dial system of rotary phones was invented by an undertaker?

Museum of Independent Telephony

412 South Campbell
Abilene, Kansas 67410
(785) 263-2681
www.heritagecenterdk.com
This museum is in the Dickinson County Heritage Center and tells the story of C. L. Brown, whose independent Brown Telephone Company of Abilene grew to become Sprint. Visitors learn about the evolution of the telephone and can role-play as an old-timey telephone operator.

WEBSITES AND ONLINE VIDEOS

Alexander Graham Bell's Obituary

www.nytimes.com/learning/general/onthisday/bday/0303.html
Read the original *New York Times* announcement of Alexander Graham Bell's death on August 3, 1922.

Telephone History

http://privateline.com
Detailed information organized by decade from Alexander Graham Bell's invention to mobile phones.

AT&T Archives

http://techchannel.att.com/index.cfm
Get a feel for how much telephone technology has changed over the years with these period videos from the 20th century.

Alexander Graham Bell

www.history.com/topics/inventions/alexander-graham-bell
This website features biographical information, pictures, speeches, and videos about the inventor.

Alexander Graham Bell's Path to the Telephone

www2.iath.virginia.edu/albell/homepage.html
This multilayered website by the Institute for Advanced Technology in the Humanities Alderman Library at the University of Virginia features a fantastic graphic flow chart of how Bell put together his knowledge of acoustics, electricity, and harmonics to invent the telephone.

Deaf: Cultures and Communication, 1600 to the Present

http://exhibits.library.yale.edu/exhibits/show/deafculture
This Yale University Library online exhibit explores the history of deaf communication and deaf culture, including the oralism vs. manualism debate that Bell was involved in.

Alexander Graham Bell

www.carnetdevol.org/Bell/biography.html
This thorough biography organized by Alexander Graham Bell's endeavors (kite building, airplanes, etc.) includes plenty of historical images.

Visible Speech

www.omniglot.com/writing/visiblespeech.htm
Interested in Melville Bell's visible speech system? This website explains the symbols and how to read them.

Helen Keller Kids Museum

http://braillebug.afb.org/hkmuseum.asp
This online museum tells the story of Helen Keller's life and includes historical photos. It was created by the American Foundation for the Blind.

Glossary

acoustics—the science of sound and sound waves

aerodrome—an airplane

aeronautics—the science of flight, especially aircraft design

aileron—a movable flap on an airplane wing used for banking, rolling, or balancing

amplitude—the height of a sound wave and measure of loudness

apparatus—a piece of machinery or a device

astronomer—a scientist who studies outer space and space objects

audiometer—an instrument for measuring ability and range of hearing

centennial—the hundredth anniversary of an event

circuit—the path an electric current flows

context—the information surrounding a word that helps determine its meaning

criterion—a standard on which a judgment or decision is based (the plural form is criteria)

current—the flow of electricity

diabetes—a medical condition, also called diabetes mellitus, in which the body produces an insufficient amount of insulin, causing elevated blood sugar

diaphragm—a thin, tight, flexible sheet of material that covers or divides something; a membrane

drag—the force acting against a body in motion

ear tube—a horn- or funnel-shaped device, also called an ear trumpet, used to direct sound into the ear of a person who is hearing impaired

eardrum—the thin membrane in the ear that carries sound waves as vibrations; it's also called the tympanic membrane or tympanum

electromagnetism—the scientific study of the interaction of electric and magnetic fields

elocution—the study or practice of careful, clear, effective public speaking

Gaelic—the ancient language of the Celts in Ireland and Scotland

graphophone—a phonograph

harmonics—the science of musical sounds

heavier-than-air craft—flying machines like airplanes and jets

hertz—the unit of measure for sound frequency

hydrodrome—a hydrofoil boat

hydrofoil—a fin just below the waterline of a boat that raises the hull out of the water at high speeds

lighter-than-air craft—flying vehicles that float in the air, like hot-air balloons and blimps

manual—done with the hands

membrane—a thin, flexible sheet of material that covers or divides something

miller—a person who owns or operates a mill that grinds grain into flour

monopoly—the complete control over the entire supply of goods or a service in a certain market by a single company or group

natural frequency—the sound frequency at which something vibrates naturally

Nova Scotia—the southeasternmost province of Canada

palate—roof of the mouth

patent—a government-granted exclusive right to an inventor to sell the invention; an official document stating the right

patent caveat—a confidential, formal declaration stating an intention to file a patent on an in-progress invention

phonautogram—the visible recording made by a phonautograph

phonautograph—a device that makes a visible record of a sound

phonograph—a turntable or record player

photophone— a telephone that sends sound vibrations with a beam of reflected light

physicist—a scientist who studies matter and energy

pitch—the up and down (climbing and diving) direction of an aircraft

receiver—a device for changing electric impulses into sound

resistance—an opposing force against electric flow

resonance—the prolonging of sound by reflection or by vibration of other objects

respirator—a machine that maintains breathing

roll—the tilt of an aircraft that effects balance and control

scarlet fever—a contagious bacterial infection, also called scarlatina, that mainly affects children and causes fever; swelling; pain in the nose, throat, and mouth; and a red rash

sound—something heard; vibrations transmitted through the air or other medium

sounder—a receiving device that converts a telegraphic message into sound

sound wave—vibrations that transmit sound

spectrograms—a graphic representation of sound; sonogram

stuttering—to repeat a sound or word while trying to speak

surname—last name or family name

transmitter—a device that converts sound waves to electric impulses

tuberculosis—a bacterial disease that infects and damages the lungs; consumption

undulating—wavelike, smooth up-and-down motion or shape

vocal cords—strips of tissue in the larynx that produce sound by vibrating

vocal physiology—the study of how the vocal organs produce sound and speech

yaw—the left and right direction of an aircraft

Notes

Introduction: An Inventive Teacher

"was thus introduced": Alexander Graham Bell, "Prehistoric Telephone Days," *National Geographic Magazine* 41, no. 3 (March 1922): 229.

1. A Curious Kid

"I was awakened": Edwin S. Grosvenor and Morgan Wesson, *Alexander Graham Bell: The Life and Times of the Man Who Invented the Telephone* (New York: Harry N. Abrams, 1997), 15.

"the sweetest expression": Tony Foster, *The Sound and the Silence: The Private Lives of Mabel and Alexander Graham Bell* (Halifax, NS: Nimbus, 1996), 8.

"My early passion for music": Bell, "Prehistoric Telephone Days," 225.

"Milton Cottage at Trinity": Alexander Graham Bell, "Notes of Early Life," *Volta Review* 12, no. 3 (June 1910): 159.

"In boyhood . . . I have spent": Alexander Graham Bell to Mabel Hubbard Bell, 6 December 1876, in Alexander Graham Bell family papers, 1834–1974, Library of Congress (hereafter cited as AGB Papers), www.loc.gov/item/magbell.03500303/.

"If only you could take": Bell, "Prehistoric Telephone Days," 239.

"It was a proud day": Bell, "Prehistoric Telephone Days," 239.

"Mr. Herdman's injunction to": Bell, "Notes of Early Life," 155.

"Alexander Bell was not": Foster, *Sound and the Silence*, 11.

"I passed through": Bell, "Notes of Early Life," 159.

"This year with my grandfather": Bell, "Prehistoric Telephone Days," 227.

"From this time forth": Bell, "Notes of Early Life," 159.

"treated as a boy again": Bell, "Notes of Early Life," 160.

"My brother . . . and I": Alexander Graham Bell, "Making a Talking Machine," undated, in AGB Papers, http://hdl.loc.gov/loc.mss/magbell.37600301.

"[Melly] undertook to make": Bell, "Making a Talking Machine."

"'Mamma, Mamma' came forth": Bell, "Making a Talking Machine."

"This, of course, was just": Bell, "Making a Talking Machine."

"The making of this talking-machine": Bell, "Making a Talking Machine."

2. Giving Voice to the Deaf

"I remember upon one occasion": Bell, "Prehistoric Telephone Days," 228.

"What are you doing, Aleck?": Robert V. Bruce. *Bell: Alexander Graham Bell and Conquest of Solitude* (Ithaca, NY: Cornell University Press, 1973), 45.

"Dear Papa": Alexander Graham Bell to Alexander Melville Bell, 24 November 1865, in AGB Papers, www.loc.gov/resource/magbell.19600301/.

"At the age of 18 years": Bell, "Prehistoric Telephone Days," 232.

"So long as Edward": Bruce, *Bell*, 53.

"He was only eighteen": Bruce, *Bell*, 53.

"determined little fellow": Bruce, *Bell*, 62.

"I well remember how often": Alexander Graham Bell to Mabel Hubbard Bell, 26 September 1875, in AGB Papers, www.loc.gov/item/magbell.03400114/.

"has perished with poor Melly": Alexander Graham Bell to Alexander Melville Bell, 5 June 1870, in AGB Papers, www.loc.gov/item/magbell.00400118/.

3. The Bell Patent Association

"It was my custom": Alexander Graham Bell to Mabel Hubbard Bell, 26 September 1875.

"paved the way for": Bell, "Prehistoric Telephone Days," 229.

"It would be possible": Alexander Graham Bell, "Dr. Bell on Telephone Discovery," *Boston City Club Bulletin* 10, (October 1915): 31.

"At once the conception": Fred DeLand, "An Ever-Continuing Memorial," *Volta Review* 24, no. 10 (October 1922): 360.

"I made stubborn metal": Thomas A. Watson, *Exploring Life: The Autobiography of Thomas A. Watson* (New York: Appleton, 1926), 35.

"a tall, slender, quick-motioned": Watson, *Exploring Life*, 54.

"I . . . was always clumsy": Bell, "Prehistoric Telephone Days," 235.

"No finer influence than": Watson, *Exploring Life*, 57.

"[Henry] said he thought": Alexander Graham Bell, *The Bell Telephone: The Deposition of Alexander Graham Bell, in the Suit Brought by the United States* (Boston: American Bell Telephone Company, 1908), 48.

"Get it!": Bell, *Bell Telephone*, 48.

"I cannot tell you": Bell, *Bell Telephone*, 48.

"increase and diffusion": James Smithson's 1826 will, Smithsonian Archives History Division, 72-3960-A and 72-3960, https://siarchives.si.edu/history /james-smithson.

"But for Joseph Henry": Thomas Coulson, *Joseph Henry: His Life and Work* (Princeton, NJ: Princeton University Press, 1950), 315.

4. "Mr. Watson—Come Here"

"Every moment of my time": Alexander Graham Bell to Alexander Melville Bell and Eliza Symonds Bell, 24 May 1875, in AGB Papers, www.loc.gov/item/magbell .00500113/.

"If I can get a mechanism": Watson, *Exploring Life*, 16.

"I have discovered": Bruce, *Bell*, 151.

"my wish to make": Alexander Graham Bell to Mabel Hubbard Bell, 8 August 1875, in AGB Papers, www.loc.gov/item/magbell.03400101/.

"he dressed badly": Bruce, *Bell*, 100.

"In spite of Bell's": Watson, *Exploring Life*, 60.

"I began to readjust": Watson, *Exploring Life*, 67.

"The speaking telephone was": Watson, *Exploring Life*, 69.

"If she does not": Helen Elmira Waite. *Make a Joyful Sound: The Romance of Mabel Hubbard and Alexander Graham Bell* (Philadelphia: Macrae Smith, 1961), 118.

"I am afraid to": Waite, *Joyful Sound*, 120–121.

"The history of the telephone": "Denies Bell Invented Telephone," *Telephony* 8, no. 1 (July 1904): 35.

"When Mr. Watson talked": Alexander Graham Bell, *Notebook by Alexander Graham Bell, from 1875 to 1876. Alexander Graham Bell family papers, 1834-1974*, Library of Congress. http://hdl.loc.gov/loc.mss/magbell.25300201/.

"Mr. Watson was stationed": Alexander Graham Bell, "Experiments Made by A. Graham Bell (Vol. I)," notebook, 1875–1876, in AGB Papers, http://hdl.loc.gov /loc.mss/magbell.25300201/.

"Articulate speech was transmitted": Alexander Graham Bell to Alexander Melville Bell, 10 March 1876, in AGB Papers, www.loc.gov/item/magbell.00500211/.

5. On the Road and on to New Inventions

"I hear, I hear!": Bruce, *Bell*, 197.

"Before long, friends will": John E. Kingsbury, *The Telephone and Telephone Exchanges: Their Invention and Development* (London: Longmans, Green, 1915), 52.

"Of what use is": Quoted in Decree for Perpetual Injunction: Circuit Court of the United States, American Bell Telephone Company vs. American Cushman Telephone Company (July 21, 1888), 19.

"Two years later those": Watson, *Exploring Life*, 107.

"I am the invisible": *The Telephone*, directed by Karen Goodman and Kirk Simon, American Experience, aired February 3, 1997, on PBS.

"What a longing I have": Mabel Hubbard Bell and Alexander Graham Bell to Eliza Symonds Bell, 14 August 1877, in AGB Papers, www.loc.gov/item /magbell.02800120/.

"most extraordinary": Bruce, *Bell*, 241.

"one of the greatest events": *Telephone*, directed by Goodman and Simon.

"The more fame a man": Alexander Graham Bell to Mabel Hubbard Bell, 9 September 1878, in AGB Papers, www.loc.gov/item/magbell.03510410/.

"The inventor is a": Alexander Graham Bell, "Aerial Locomotion," speech, 4 March 1907, in AGB Papers, www.loc.gov/item/magbell.37500101/.

"business (which is hateful": Alexander Graham Bell to Gardiner Greene Hubbard, 28 October 1877, in AGB Papers, www.loc.gov/item/magbell.07900417/.

"I can't bear to": Alexander Graham Bell to Mabel Hubbard Bell, 5 April 1879, in AGB Papers, www.loc.gov/item/magbell.03600212/.

"Discoveries and inventions arise": Alexander Graham Bell, "Discovery and Invention," *National Geographic Magazine* 25, no. 6 (June 1914): 654.

"I have heard articulate": Alexander Graham Bell to Alexander Melville Bell, 26 February 1880, in AGB Papers, www.loc.gov/item/magbell.00510307/.

"The whole world watched": Alexander Graham Bell, "An Induction Balance," *American Journal of Science* 25, no. 145 (January–June 1883): 22.

"Certainly no man can": Grosvenor and Wesson, *Alexander Graham Bell*, 108.

"Poor little one": Bruce, *Bell*, 317.

6. Understanding for Everyone

"I have been so": Alexander Graham Bell to Mabel Hubbard Bell, 9 September 1878.

"Who can picture the": December 12, 1887, speech, quoted in Bruce, *Bell*, 379.

"advocating independence through": AG Bell Association, "Mission," www.facebook.com/pg/AGBellAssociation/about/.

"ASL is the backbone": "American Sign Language," National Association of the Deaf, www.nad.org/resources/american-sign-language/.

"Bell was never happier": Helen Keller, *The Story of My Life* (New York: Doubleday, 1903), 137.

"That interview would be": Keller, *Story of My Life*, 19.

"Dear Mr. Bell": Keller, *Story of My Life*, 148–149.

"You can never imagine": Keller, *Story of My Life*, 217.

"He makes you feel": Keller, *Story of My Life*, 137.

"One would think I had": Foster, *Sound and the Silence*, 134.

"recognition of my work": Robert V. Bruce, "A Conquest of Solitude," *American Heritage* 24, no. 3 (April 1973), www.americanheritage.com/content/conquest-solitude.

"In scientific researches": Lawrence Surtees, "Bell, Alexander Graham," *Dictionary of Canadian Biography*, vol. 15 (Toronto, ON: University of Toronto/Université Laval, 2003), www.biographi.ca/en/bio/bell_alexander_graham_15E.html.

"I am a graphophone": Grosvenor and Wesson, *Alexander Graham Bell*, 111.

"The world and all that": Grosvenor and Wesson, *Alexander Graham Bell*, 190.

7. Into the Air, Water, and History

"My name is Alexander": Grosvenor and Wesson, *Alexander Graham Bell*, 137.

"Beautiful dense woods of fir": Mabel Hubbard Bell to Eliza Symonds Bell, 21 August 1886, in AGB Papers, www.loc.gov/item/magbell.02800608/.

"Though I cannot claim": Surtees, "Bell, Alexander Graham."

"the possibility of making": Watson, *Exploring Life*, 153.

"as soon as the telephone": Watson, *Exploring Life*, 154.

"revolution in the world's": Cleveland Moffet, "The Edge of the Future: An Interview with Prof. Alexander Graham Bell," *McClure's Magazine*, 1 (June 1893), 39.

"Langley's flying machines": Alexander Graham Bell to Mabel Hubbard Bell, 15 June 1891, in AGB Papers, www.loc.gov/item/magbell.03710311/.

"I must confess that": Alexander Graham Bell to Mabel Hubbard Bell, 9 May 1895, in AGB Papers, www.loc.gov/item/magbell.03900205/.

"It resembled an enormous bird": A. Graham Bell and S. P. Langley, "A Successful Trial of the Aerodrome," *Science* 3, no. 73 (22 May 1896): 753–754, DOI: 10.1126/science.3.73.753.

"No one could have": Bell and Langley, "Successful Trial."

"A dead man tells no tales": Alexander Graham Bell, journal from September 2, 1901, to October 29, 1901, in AGB Papers, www.loc.gov/item/magbell.21600201/.

"I have been continuously": Alexander Graham Bell, "The Tetrahedral Principle in Kite Structure," *National Geographic Magazine* 14, no. 6 (June 1903): 219.

"If a kite flies well": Alexander Graham Bell, "The Tetrahedral Principle in Kite Structure," *National Geographic Magazine* 14, no. 6 (June 1903): 220.

"He goes up there": Surtees, "Bell, Alexander Graham."

"Mr. Bell has nothing": Bruce, *Bell*, 407.

"It began to pull": Keller, *Story of My Life*, 278.

"I believe [the tetrahedron]": Bruce, *Bell*, 433.

"Hurrah for Curtiss!": Jean Lesage, "Alexander Graham Bell Museum Tribute to Genius," *National Geographic Magazine* 110, no. 2 (August 1956): 252.

"we drove home at night": Bruce, *Bell*, 453.

"Quick as a flash": Marvin W. McFarland, ed., *The Papers of Wilbur and Orville Wright* (New York: McGraw-Hill, 2000), 937.

"Let's hold tight together": Mabel Hubbard Bell to Alexander Graham Bell, 20 September 1908, in AGB Papers, www.loc.gov/item/magbell.04300136/.

"Mr. Watson, come here": Watson, *Exploring Life*, 309.

"It would take me": Watson, *Exploring Life*, 309.

"The telephone has gone": Bell, "Prehistoric Telephone Days," 241.

"[The inventor] is haunted": Lesage, "Museum Tribute," 232.

"over Lake Maggiore at": Bruce, *Bell*, 467.

"At fifteen knots": Bruce, *Bell*, 474.

"Leave the beaten track": Bell, "Discovery and Invention," 654.

Bibliography

Alexander Graham Bell Family Papers. Library of Congress. www.loc.gov/collections/alexander-graham-bell-papers/.

Bell, A. Graham, and S. P. Langley. "A Successful Trial of the Aerodrome." *Science* 3, no. 73 (22 May 1896): 753–754. DOI: 10.1126/science.3.73.753.

Bell, Alexander Graham. *The Bell Telephone: The Deposition of Alexander Graham Bell, in the Suit Brought by the United States.* Boston: American Bell Telephone Company, 1908.

Bell, Alexander Graham. "Discovery and Invention." *National Geographic Magazine* 25, no. 6 (June 1914): 649–655.

Bell, Alexander Graham. "Dr. Bell on Telephone Discovery." *Boston City Club Bulletin* 10 (October 1915): 31.

Bell, Alexander Graham. "An Induction Balance." *American Journal of Science* 25, no. 145 (Jan–June 1883): 22.

Bell, Alexander Graham. "Notes of Early Life." *Volta Review* 12, no. 3 (June 1910): 155.

Bell, Alexander Graham. "Prehistoric Telephone Days." *National Geographic Magazine* 41, no. 3 (March 1922): 223–241.

Bell, Alexander Graham. "The Tetrahedral Principle in Kite Structure." *National Geographic Magazine* 14, no. 6 (June 1903): 220.

Bruce, Robert V. *Bell: Alexander Graham Bell and Conquest of Solitude.* Ithaca, NY: Cornell University Press, 1973.

Bruce, Robert V. "A Conquest of Solitude." *American Heritage* 24, no. 3 (April 1973). www.americanheritage.com/content/conquest-solitude.

Cochrane, William, John Castell Hopkins, and W. J. Hunter, *The Canadian Album: Men of Canada, Vol. 4: 1891–1896.* Bradley, Garretson, 1891.

Coulson, Thomas. *Joseph Henry: His Life and Work.* Princeton, NJ: Princeton University Press, 1950.

DeLand, Fred. "An Ever-Continuing Memorial." *Volta Review* 24, no. 10 (October 1922): 360.

"Denies Bell Invented Telephone." *Telephony* 8, no. 1 (July 1904): 35.

Foster, Tony. *The Sound and the Silence: The Private Lives of Mabel and Alexander Graham Bell.* Halifax, NS: Nimbus, 1996.

Grosvenor, Edwin S., and Morgan Wesson. *Alexander Graham Bell: The Life and Times of the Man Who Invented the Telephone.* New York: Harry N. Abrams, 1997.

Keller, Helen. *The Story of My Life.* New York: Doubleday, 1903.

Kingsbury, John E. *The Telephone and Telephone Exchanges: Their Invention and Development.* London: Longmans, Green, 1915.

Lesage, Jean. "Alexander Graham Bell Museum Tribute to Genius." *National Geographic Magazine* 110, no. 2 (August 1956): 227–256.

McFarland, Marvin W., ed. *The Papers of Wilbur and Orville Wright.* New York: McGraw-Hill, 2000.

Moffet, Cleveland. "The Edge of the Future: An Interview with Prof. Alexander Graham Bell." *McClure's Magazine* 1 (June 1893), 39–43.

Surtees, Lawrence. "Bell, Alexander Graham." *Dictionary of Canadian Biography.* Vol. 15. Toronto, ON: University of Toronto/Université Laval, 2003. www.biographi.ca/en/bio/bell_alexander_graham_15E.html.

Waite, Helen Elmira. *Make a Joyful Sound: The Romance of Mabel Hubbard and Alexander Graham Bell.* Philadelphia: Macrae Smith, 1961.

Watson, Thomas A. *Exploring Life: The Autobiography of Thomas A. Watson.* New York: Appleton, 1926.

Index

Page numbers in italics refer to photos.

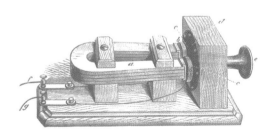